January 2012

To My lovely brother

Happy Birthday

with love

Angela
x.

CW00820628

All Around Anglesey

To the memory of my friend
Gwyn Pari Huws

Published in 2007 by
Gomer Press, Llandysul, Ceredigion, SA44 4JL
www.gomer.co.uk

ISBN 978 1 84323 715 0

A CIP record for this title is available from the British Library.
Copyright © Terry Beggs, 2007

The author asserts his moral right under the Copyright, Designs
and Patents Act, 1988 to be identified as author of this work.

This book is published with the financial support
of the Welsh Books Council.

Printed and bound in Wales at
Gomer Press, Llandysul, Ceredigion

All Around Anglesey

Terry Beggs

Gomer

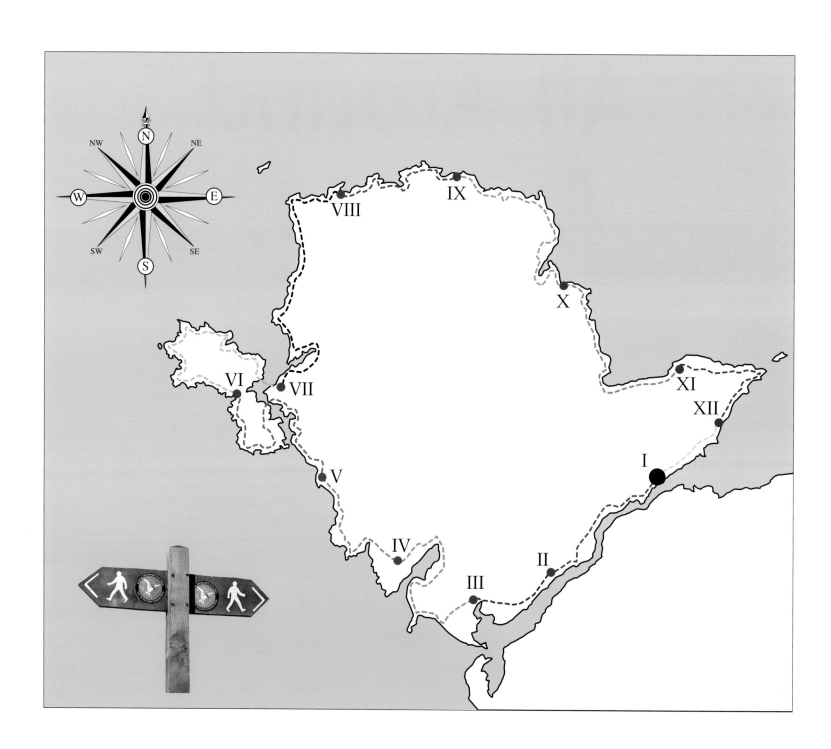

CONTENTS

Foreword

This book is dedicated to my father. He would have been honoured and delighted. The Anglesey coast was important to him; it was on the Menai Strait, on board HMS *Conway* that he prepared for a career at sea; it was at the opposite end of the island that he taught my brothers and me to sail, and where as a family we spent holidays swimming, fishing and messing around in boats; and it was to the coast of Anglesey that he returned to sail following his retirement.

I still explore Anglesey's coastline, on foot, under sail and paddling my kayak. Readers of this wonderful book will understand why the island has such a hold on so many of us. Terry Beggs has captured Ynys Môn's beauty in both words and pictures. *All Around Anglesey* will doubtless spur the active into following in his footsteps, but will comfort armchair explorers, for they too can share this memorable journey.

Siân Pari Huws

Introduction

It has been my good fortune to spend a large part of my life in Anglesey and, now that we have retired, my wife and I live only a furlong from Afon Cadnant, overlooking the Menai Strait. For me, there is nowhere in the world more attractive than Ynys Môn. As a home, a place to explore or simply to visit, the Isle of Anglesey has so much to offer: a wonderful coastline, magnificent scenery, endless sea and sky, fresh air, superb beaches, birds and marine life, delightful villages and acres of rolling farmland – everything, in fact, except a respectable range of mountains. Even these are only a few miles distant on the north Wales mainland.

Anglesey has a long and interesting history, reflected in both its archaeology and in some of the finest geology in the British Isles. Despite its small population – under 70,000 – the island also seems to have produced more than its fair share of gifted and scholarly people.

Getting to know the island takes time, of course. Wandering along the lanes and beaches, it is easy to imagine how little has changed here in hundreds of years and it is this quality of timelessness that makes Anglesey such a relaxing and special environment. And if it has always been like this, then there seems to be little point in the island drawing attention to itself by any artificial means. Indeed, but for the efforts of a few local people wishing to share their island, this delightful north-west corner of Wales might easily be overlooked.

Some years ago now, my shipping industry friend and colleague, Gwyn Pari Huws, sadly no longer with us, suggested that we might produce a book about the magical waterway that separates Anglesey from the mainland. Our research brought us enormous pleasure: making passages in various craft between Llanddwyn Island and Puffin Island, as well as walking the shorelines, collecting information and taking photographs. The resulting book *Y Fenai* or *The Menai Strait* inspired me to think of another project in which the camera could play a leading role. The completion of Anglesey's 125-mile coastal path opened up just such an opportunity. My idea was to walk the entire circuit clockwise – a purely personal preference – time and weather permitting, taking photographs and making notes along the way.

The walk was an entertaining and exhilarating experience and included stretches of coastline completely new to me. Operating alone, at an average of five miles per day, the project took me from February to October during 2004, but with so much to occupy my thoughts and to keep the camera busy, the miles rolled away beneath my feet. Because the coastal path was the lynchpin to the whole project, it was important that the majority of my photographs should be taken either from or close to the path. Far from being a restriction, this allowed me to indulge my interest in the island's geology and its maritime connections, enough material for several books!

Anglesey's coastal path is a splendid development, well-engineered, maintained and signposted. It follows the island's perimeter sensibly, but it is seldom far from the 'edge' and therefore walkers should remain alert. The few inland detours only serve to enrich the experience. The creators, managers and maintainers of the path deserve congratulation and, should its status be elevated to that of a National Trail, theirs will be the reward. Lastly, I should make it clear that this book is not intended to serve as an authoritative guide. It is simply an account of what, for me, was a most rewarding and memorable walk. If it draws attention to the variety, interest and incredible beauty of Anglesey's coastline, it will have served its purpose. Better still, if my enjoyment of the coastal path encourages others to venture forth; that will be my reward.

Some practical notes

If you are contemplating the coastal path circuit, or even part of it, the official pack 'A Guide to the Isle of Anglesey Coastal Path' is a MUST. It contains information relevant to your planning stages, together with twelve attractive section maps which display, in addition to the route itself, a wealth of practical information. It is on sale at the Tourist Information Centre, 01248 713177, next to the railway station in Llanfair Pwllgwyngyll.

To follow your route with certainty, you are advised to carry an Ordnance Survey map, (Landranger 114 or Explorer 262 and 263), in addition to the guide. A compass and Lavers Liverpool & Irish Sea Tide Table would also be useful. Please do pay attention to weather forecasts and take a mobile telephone with you, preferably switched off!

Terry Beggs,
Menai Bridge

I From Menai Bridge to Llanidan

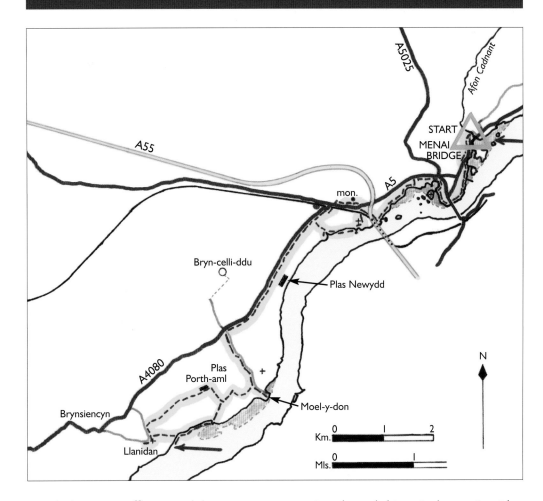

In which we get off to an exhilarating start, passing through historical Menai Bridge and enjoying close encounters with the two famous bridges that bracket the infamous Swellies. We pass by 'the village with the longest name' and the home of the Marquess of Anglesey, learn about two famous Merchant Navy training establishments and look across the Strait to Y Felinheli.

The Cadnant estuary at low tide in midwinter

Anglesey's early settlers would have crossed the Strait to reach the Island and so our walk 'All Around Anglesey' begins where the Iron Age tribes-people would have landed, at the mouth of Afon Cadnant, *en route* to their Llanddyfnan settlement between present-day Pentraeth and Talwrn.

Two bridges cross Afon Cadnant, the old stone bridge in its picturesque setting and its concrete and steel replacement, more suited to modern traffic, carrying the A545 to Beaumaris. To the south-west lies Menai Bridge, heralded by an increasing number of waterside dwellings, looking out upon the Strait's 'islands' of Gaint and Faelog. What is known today as Menai Bridge town was originally Porthaethwy, principal port in medieval times of the Tindaethwy Hundred, that large division of Anglesey land that included most of the Menai shoreline. But the construction of the suspension bridge, by far the greatest event in the town's history, put it squarely 'on the map', and so, whether by design or just common usage, it is hardly surprising that Porthaethwy became known as 'Menai Bridge' as well. The fact that both names are still in regular use today is both interesting and historically appealing.

On our left, a small sign advertises the Tegfryn Gallery and this should be noted for two reasons. Firstly, because the next turning left into St Georges Road leads back to the waterfront, and secondly because the works of several local and renowned artists are displayed in this elegant house and deserve an unhurried return visit. St Georges Road leads down to handsome Victorian terraces overlooking the little port but, in turn, they are overlooked by the large functional buildings of the University's School of Ocean Sciences. The School's continual expansion, from its early beginnings in the 1950s, reflects the importance of its work and its growing international reputation. The new research vessel *Prince Madog*, specially designed to operate in the Irish Sea and sometimes further afield, is a familiar sight here as Menai Bridge is its 'home port'.

A small iron gate almost opposite the Mostyn Arms gives access to a pleasant promenade area associated with the rebuilt St George's Pier. Its floating pontoon provides a berth for *Prince Madog* as well as, in season, various pleasure craft and work boats. From this pier, the view towards Telford's bridge includes Prince's Pier and the quay at Porth Daniel, where square-rigged Scandinavian timber ships once lay to discharge their cargoes. Today the same quay serves as a parking space for showy fibre-glass motor boats. At a T-junction outside the Liverpool Arms, the road from the town square on the right bears the Welsh name Stryd-y-Paced. In years gone by, this was the route down to the pier to join the packet steamers for passage to Liverpool.

Continuing south-westwards, there's a public slipway at Porth Wrach (Witches' Cove), a bowling green and several interesting properties lining the route, including the old courthouse. Upon reaching Porth Lladron (Thieves' Cove), however, all attention switches immediately to the magnificent suspension bridge spanning the Strait. Towering aloft, Telford's beautifully engineered masonry and ironwork is quite breathtaking.

The site of Telford's workshop lies in the trees to the left and his residence, now called Summer Court, hides away on the opposite side of the narrow road. The Belgian Promenade, that follows the foreshore and links Carreg-yr-Halen to Ynys Tysilio's causeway, was built by a group of Belgian refugees who, having been driven from their home town Mechelen during the German invasion, were provided with food and shelter in the town of Menai Bridge. Opened in 1916,

The Belgian Promenade

the Promenade marked two years of labour and was a gesture of appreciation to the hospitable townspeople, providing them with a delightful Strait-side walk.

A trip across the causeway to Ynys Tysilio (Church Island), is a small but rewarding diversion. Saint Tysilio was alive in the sixth century and the tiny church, built in the fifteenth century, is dedicated to his memory. Local people who worked as fishermen and ferrymen in these dangerous waters number among those buried in this picturesque setting. A climb up to the War Memorial reveals a splendid view of the treacherous Swellies (Pwll Ceris), with its islets, rocks and turbulent tides, all the way to the Britannia Bridge.

For a short distance westward, the walk joins and follows part of the original London to Holyhead A5 coaching route. It is tempting to imagine teams of

horses drawing their coaches, full of Dublin-bound passengers. Where the coastal path returns to the shoreline, near the time of slack water, various pleasure craft may be seen negotiating the narrow channel; how different from the numerous cargo-laden schooners in the eighteenth and nineteenth centuries!

The Swellies, that mile of waterway between the two bridges, can display moods ranging from tranquillity to sheer violence. On a sunny day with a neap tide and with ducks and geese cruising in the shallows, there are few sights more attractive, but with a south-west gale blowing in opposition to a big spring ebb, the Swellies become decidedly hostile and dangerous. Boiling overfalls and eddies abound and the racing tidal stream claws at the little cottage on Ynys Gorad Goch. Over the years a number of vessels have been lost in the Swellies, perhaps the most famous being the Merchant Navy's cadet training ship HMS *Conway* in 1953. Caught by the strong tide while under tow from her mooring off Plas Newydd for a refit in Birkenhead, the tug's towrope parted under the strain and the old 'Wooden Wall' was swept onto the Platters, a rock ledge just 400 yards from the suspension bridge. Hard aground, her end was nigh for, as the tide fell, she broke her back over the edge of the Platters.

The sheer power of the surging water is awesome and yet, in years gone by and for those who understood its ways, the Swellies provided a livelihood, as is evident in the remains of several stone-built fish traps along its Anglesey shore and on Ynys Gorad Goch itself. Herring was the main catch in those days; the fish were carried into the traps by the tidal stream and, being averse to swimming against the six-knot flow, they were stranded and then collected as the water level fell. A hundred years ago, the family occupying the island cottage supplemented their living by offering a 'Gorad Tea' consisting of fried whitebait, brown bread and butter and a pot of tea, all for a shilling! Customers summoned the island's boat by ringing a bell hung from a tree in Coed Môr and, having enjoyed their tea, were doubtless invited to buy some smoked fish from the little island's smokery before returning home.

The A5 London to Holyhead coaching route

The suspension bridge, and Ynys Gorad Goch

Crossings to Anglesey

Travelling to Anglesey a few centuries ago was not a journey to be undertaken lightly. A passage in a cargo schooner would be uncertain, even dangerous; to journey along north Wales' inadequate roads and then to cross the Menai Strait demanded both stamina and nerve.

Having crossed the River Conwy, travellers from the east, particularly those on foot, would often seek the most direct route to Anglesey via the Beaumaris ferry. This meant dropping down onto the Lafan Sands near Penmaen-mawr, walking to the water's edge opposite Beaumaris, and then attempting to summon the ferry. The three-mile walk across featureless sands had to be carefully timed so as to follow the receding ebb tide and reach the boarding point before low water, for if the ferry failed to materialise, a rapid retreat to the mainland would be required to avoid being overtaken by the next flood tide; a hazardous ordeal, particularly if a sea fog rolled in!

Those travelling by coach from London to Dublin would be taken to Porthaethwy, by far the busiest crossing, with ferries to deal with all manner of traffic. Already weary from their three-day journey, passengers were filled with foreboding by the prospect of the narrow but dangerous Strait. Not only did people question the seaworthiness of the ferries, for it was known there had been a number of accidents here in the strong tides and funnelling winds (with serious loss of life), but also the ferry operators were notorious for their extortionate practices.

Perhaps there was a more domestic feel to the ferries further west along the Strait, particularly at Moel-y-don, Tal-y-foel and Abermenai, which were used more by local people than travellers: going to work, going shopping and even going to school.

Telford's suspension bridge

timewatch

1819

The foundation stone of Thomas Telford's suspension bridge for horse-drawn carriages and pedestrians was laid on 10 August.

1826

The suspension bridge opening ceremony was led by the London to Holyhead stagecoach and a procession of coaches, including engineers, contractors and Telford himself.

1850

Following an Act of Parliament and exhaustive testing of George and Robert Stephenson's revolutionary design, the foundation stone of the Britannia rail bridge was finally laid on 10 April 1846. The bridge opened in 1850, when Robert Stephenson hammered in the last rivet and then rode across Pont Britannia in a train carrying 1,000 passengers and drawn by three locomotives.

1980

The Prince of Wales declared the new Britannia rail AND road bridge open on 11 July, following ten years of reconstruction after the disastrous fire of 1970.

THE MENAI SUSPENSION BRIDGE

The Act of Union with Ireland brought complaints from influential voices about the roads of north Wales and the Menai Strait ferries. These resulted in the appointment of civil engineer Thomas Telford as the Holyhead Road Engineer, with the purpose of bridging the Strait. Inevitably the ferrymen opposed the plan and, with 4,000 commercial vessels using the Strait annually, the Admiralty demanded a clearance of 100 feet above high water and no hindrance to navigation. Eventually, Telford's design for two carriageways separated by a pedestrian walkway, all suspended from chains in a single span across the Strait, was accepted.

While stone masons built the two limestone towers and landward arches, sixteen wrought-iron chains were forged, each 1,714 feet long and weighing 121 tons. Anchored in rock, the chains were led over cast-iron saddles on top of the towers; the most difficult operation was connecting up the first central section of chain. This was achieved by laying out the 590-foot chain on a long narrow raft and floating it into position. Finally, thirty-two men were needed to hoist the ends, using tackles and capstans.

With the carriageway connected to the chains by vertical iron rods and the toll houses installed, the bridge was complete.

THE BRITANNIA TUBULAR BRIDGE

Long before automobiles, engineer George Stephenson of *Rocket* fame was commissioned to build a route for the 'Irish Mail' train, across the Menai Strait to Holyhead. With the help of his son Robert, Stephenson's bridge design employed the 'box girder' principle whereby twin rail tracks would pass through parallel wrought-iron tubes, supported only at their ends by masonry towers. The design raised eyebrows but was accepted.

Huge limestone towers were built on opposite sides of the Strait, with a third one in the middle, upon Carreg Frydan. Meanwhile, an army of artisans built the four long tubes to span the Strait, each one 472 feet long, 25 feet tall, 15 feet wide, weighing 1,500 tons and containing 325,000 rivets! Two twenty-ton stone lions placed at each end of the bridge completed the construction.

Britannia Bridge operated satisfactorily for 120 years but, on 23 May 1970, its timber-lined tubes were severely damaged by fire. In its reconstruction, the famous tubes were sacrificed but the lions survived!

The Marquess of Anglesey by moonlight

A stone lion (one of four) guards the Britannia Bridge

The Toll House next to first home of the Women's Institute

A quarter-mile beyond Ynys Gorad Goch stands Robert Stephenson's famous Britannia Bridge, rebuilt in 1980 to carry both rail and road traffic. Here the path turns inland and climbs up between the railway embankment and Carreg Môn Hotel. In a little while the path forms a T-junction with a narrow road and there is a choice of onward route: right, up the hill or left, under the railway bridge, and down through St Mary's churchyard with its small monument to the memory of those who lost their lives while building the Britannia Bridge. At the shoreline, a statue of Admiral Lord Nelson unexpectedly comes into view, standing upon rocks at the water's edge, gazing seaward. The statue was created in 1875, some seventy years after the Battle of Trafalgar, by no less a person than Admiral Lord Clarence Paget who lived and pursued

his talent for sculpture at the mansion of Plas Llanfair just visible among the trees, a quarter mile ahead. His Lordship's competent sculpture has undoubted presence but it seems that he may have underestimated its weight, for the story goes that it took a team of thirty-two horses to drag the statue to its plinth.

About a mile and a half south-west from the statue, occupying a clearing in the deciduous woodland of the Anglesey shoreline, is another Paget mansion. This very fine residence, Plas Newydd, is the home of the Marquess of Anglesey. The mansion and its superb estate are now in the hands of the National Trust.

A better view of Plas Llanfair, a building with an unusual history, is to be had further along the stony beach. During the 1930s it became a hotel before being requisitioned in 1939 for the use of American servicemen. Then, in 1945, the mansion and its grounds were purchased to provide a permanent base for a boys' boarding school which had strong nautical traditions and connections. Originally founded in 1864 aboard HMS *Indefatigable*, moored in the River Mersey, the school provided an education and pre-sea training for boys destined to go to sea as Merchant Navy ratings, but enemy action over Liverpool forced its relocation to Plas Llanfair for the boys' safety. The school finally closed in 1995, at which point the estate was taken over by the Ministry of Defence to provide a joint services training centre. A high security fence was erected but, happily, the name 'Indefatigable' was retained.

Once past 'Indefatigable', the route follows a stone walkway beside the sea wall, climbs over a stone jetty outside the Commandant's house and enters a tranquil and charming creek known as Pwllfanogl. The few attractive properties here, one of which was the home and studio of the late Sir Kyffin Williams RA, give hardly a hint of the industry that existed at Pwllfanogl until about a hundred years ago, when vessels moored up to the little stone quay to discharge and load their cargoes. Wood-framed slates for infant pupils were among the products assembled and shipped out from here. Perhaps, some readers remember learning to write on these with their slate pencils?

The coastal path now leads inland again and up to the A4080. The alternative route, up the hill from the T-junction outside Carreg Môn Hotel, leads back up to the A5 where a tall monument stands upon a rare outcrop of dark blue glaucophane schist, a metamorphic rock of Precambrian age. The monument is known as the 'Marquess of Anglesey's Column' and presides over the A5 towards the village of Llanfairpwll. It was erected to the memory of Henry William Paget, the first Marquess of Anglesey, a title awarded in recognition of his bravery at the Battle of Waterloo. Spectacular views of the Menai Strait, its surrounding countryside and the mountains of Snowdonia await those intrepid visitors prepared to climb the 115 steps to the column's lofty observation platform. The village beneath the Marquess's bronzed gaze is famous for having the longest name in the British Isles, if not the whole world:

Llanfairpwllgwyngyllgogerychwyrndrobwll-
llantysiliogogogoch.

Plas Porth-aml

It was bound to claim the attention of travellers passing this way, for the name is extremely descriptive: 'The Church of St Mary in the hollow of the White Hazel near the fierce Whirlpool and the Church of Tysilio by the Red Cave'. But the village has more than one claim to fame, for in the corrugated-iron hall adjacent to Telford's Toll House, the first-ever meeting of the Women's Institute in Britain took place in 1915. Surprisingly, the driving force behind this development was a man, the Hon RSG Stapleton-Cotton, whose wife became the WI's first President in Britain.

The road (A4080) now follows the high limestone perimeter wall of the Plas Newydd estate until a gateway provides an entrance for visitors, via the National Trust's ticket office. The gardens and the mansion house, steeped in history, are well worth a visit. Sadly, however, visitors are unlikely to be made aware that the Marquess graciously provided

accommodation in his north wing, stables and other buildings for the junior cadets of HMS *Conway* from 1949, and for all 300 of the officer cadets from 1953 following the loss of their ship. This famous Merchant Navy training school closed in 1975.

More limestone wall to follow, all the way to the Llanddaniel crossroads, but with splendid fields and mature hardwoods to the right. After a left turn at the crossroads, the last mile to Moel-y-don is downhill, passing Llanedwen church on the way. (Right at the crossroads would lead to Bryn-celli-ddu, a large Stone Age chambered burial mound dating from about 3,000 years BC.) The Moel-y-don ferry to Y Felinheli, once an important link for Anglesey men employed at the Dinorwig slate quarry, was the last Strait ferry to cease regular operations, in 1958; but the stone jetty and attractive waterside cottages remain.

A narrow lane meanders south-westward through farmland, passing isolated homesteads and a farm on its way. Half a mile along the lane, a track continues south-westward across the fields to the shore of the Strait but, if the tide is high, it is better to turn right and stay with the lane to Plas Porth-aml, bearing left at the duck pond. Then another mile of easy walking along a lane between fields, muddy at times, leads to the historical hamlet of Llanidan, set among magnificent trees and rather special in some indefinable way.

Under the right tidal conditions, the route along the beach offers more extensive views, maybe even of youngsters under instruction in flotillas of small sailing craft from the Welsh Water-sports Centre at Plas Menai, across the Strait. The beach is stony, much of it local limey-sandstone of the Carboniferous era, but many of the cobbles and boulders do not 'belong', having been carried to these parts and deposited by an ice sheet during the last ice age. Before leaving the beach and ascending the track to Llanidan, this first stage of the walk ends on a happy note, with a glance at the charming little waterside residence that has been converted from Plas Llanidan's old boathouse, sheltered from the prevailing south-westerlies by its own private coppice.

Sheep chilling out!

Cottages at Moel-y-don

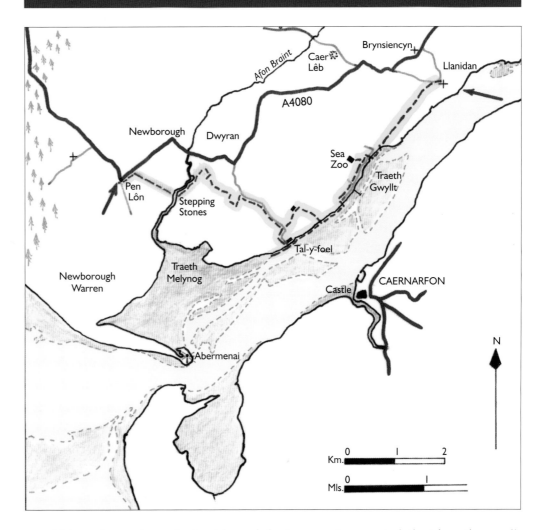

In which we learn about the Druids and the Romans in mystical Llanidan, then walk through farmland, visit a very fine Sea Zoo, reflect upon the Tal-y-foel ferry route to Caernarfon, with its famous castle set against the hills of Snowdonia, and make a unique river crossing via a line of massive stepping stones.

Wild garlic

Bodowyr burial chamber

Sheep wool

There is something mystical about Llanidan. Except for the calls of rooks and pheasants, a silence pervades; is there still a Druidic presence here? Llanidan today comprises a large mansion house, several lesser dwellings, a farm and a church founded by Saint Nidan in AD 616. Two modest roads and a lane, lined by mature chestnut, lime and beech trees, converge on a triangle of grass marked by white-painted stones outside the locked gate of the little church, no longer in regular use; but a peep over the wall reveals its long ecclesiastical past in the shape of old abbey ruins dating back to the Middle Ages when Llanidan was associated with the priory at Beddgelert.

The present Llanidan parish church of 1843 stands on higher ground on the outskirts of the village of Brynsiencyn, but coastal-path walkers do not see the village and they may not be aware of the violence that overtook the parish in AD 61 when Roman infantry under Suetonius Paulinus crossed the Strait in their flat-bottomed boats and, after fierce fighting, eventually wiped out this last stronghold of Ancient Britain, and stamped out the Druid religion. Clear evidence of its early history surrounds Brynsiencyn, prominent examples being Caer Lêb, a defended hutted enclosure which was occupied during the second half of the first millenium BC, and the Bodowyr burial chamber comprising three large stone uprights sunk into the ground as supports for a huge horizontal stone measuring eight feet by six feet. It is evident that the residents of Brynsiencyn and district go back a long way!

From a stone stile opposite the farm entrance at Llanidan, the coastal path sets off diagonally across a large field and leads to a similar stile into a coppice. Beyond the trees, the route crosses four or five more fields, passing in front of the conspicuous and stately mansion of Plas Trefarthen, until it reaches 'Barras', a striking house at the north-east corner of the shore road. There is magnificence in the distant views of the snow-topped mountains on the mainland but, nearer to hand, the prospect, though less dramatic, is equally captivating. Here grazing ponies, sheep and cattle provide subjects for the keen photographer, together with almost unnoticed detail along the walls, fences and in gateways.

Fish at the Sea Zoo

The next mile along the shore road has many points of interest. There are delightful views directly across the Strait to Waterloo Port and to Caernarfon, with its dominant Edward I castle. The views keep altering as tide levels change: a falling tide reveals the old wooden Tal-y-foel ferry landing-stage, and then the large expanse of Traeth Gwyllt sandbank and lastly, evidence of oyster beds being worked by 'Menai Oysters' of Dwyran. Situated on the other side of the road is one of Anglesey's major visitor attractions – the Sea Zoo. As its name suggests, its principal exhibits are fish and other marine life occupying their 'natural' habitats, but it also breeds lobsters and produces sea salt marketed under the name 'Halen Môn'. Further on, Foel Farm Park provides another tourist centre with its many attractions: animals, farm activities, a bistro and hand-made chocolates!

At the very end of the shore road, the small dock and what used to be 'The Mermaid Inn' probably owed their existence to the proximity of the Tal-y-foel ferry-link with Caernarfon. The original ferry crossing was from Tal-y-foel itself, about a mile further along the Strait. However, subsequent movement of the sandbanks resulted in its relocation here, to the channel inside Traeth Gwyllt, though the ferry retained the 'Tal-y-foel' name until its closure in 1953. Today, however, the dock and adjacent property are in private hands, while the old inn has responded to changing times and has become Mermaid Holiday Cottages.

The route now follows the stony beach, with a cliff of glacial deposits for company on the landward side. Views across and along the Strait are still spectacular. Quarter of a mile further on, a narrow stepped path leads up the slope to a stile and then to a track crossing two large fields. On reaching the stile at Cae Mawr farm, a lane to the left leads down to the Talgwynedd road. An alternative to the Cae Mawr route, if the tide allows, continues along the beach to the Tal-y-foel Stud Farm and Riding Centre at the end of Talgwynedd Road. (And even further along the beach lies a neat little private dock at Plas Penrhyn where there is a subtle change in the underlying Carboniferous rock, now strongly biased towards red sandstone.)

Druids and Romans

'I thought on the day when the bands of Suetonius crossed the Menai strait in their broad-bottomed boats, fell upon the Druids and their followers, who with wild looks and brandished torches lined the shore, slew hundreds with merciless butchery upon the plains, and pursued the remainder to the remotest fastnesses of the isle. I figured to myself long-bearded men with white vestments toiling up the rocks, followed by fierce warriors with glittering helms and short broad two-edged swords; I thought I heard groans, cries of rage, and the dull, awful sound of bodies precipitated down rocks.'

George Borrow, *Wild Wales*

GEORGE HENRY BORROW

✠ Born 5 July 1803 at East Dereham, Norfolk

✠ Studied law, although languages and literature became his chief interests

✠ In 1825 began first major European walking tour in France and Germany

✠ Travelled extensively to Russia, Portugal, Spain, Morocco and modern Turkey

✠ Acted as agent of the British Bible Society

✠ Cherished lifelong sympathy for native and nomadic peoples, especially gypsies

✠ Undertook walking tours in Wales and the home countries

✠ Published *Wild Wales* in 1862

✠ Died 26 July 1881

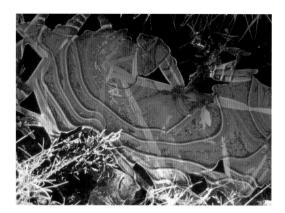

Inland now, up the Talgwynedd road for about three quarters of a mile until coastal-path signs point southwards for a little way and then north-westward, the route eventually descending to a marshy stream after about a mile. There are several attractive cottages and one or two farms along the way, colourful lichens on the stone walls and, in the distance, the scattered houses of Dwyran. On reaching the stream, the path turns south-westwards again along its bank until it merges with Afon Braint.

Having risen in a marsh near Llanddona, twelve miles distant and only a mile from Red Wharf Bay, Afon Braint flows all the way to Traeth Melynog before entering the Strait near Abermenai. Geological research has revealed that, many thousands of years ago, Afon Braint was one of two rivers involved in the formation of the Menai Strait. Following somewhat different courses in those days, the two rivers flowed towards the geological fault along whose axis the Strait now lies. (In the geological sense, a 'fault' describes a split in the rocks of the Earth's crust such that the rocks on one side of the split either move up, down or sideways relative to those on the other side.) On reaching the slight valley created by the fault, Afon Braint turned south-west while Afon Cadnant turned north-east, each deepening its channel along the fault line. However, a barrier of relatively high ground in the vicinity of today's Swellies kept the two rivers apart.

And so it remained until the ice ages when, perhaps 18,000 years ago as the ice began to melt, the melt-water found its escape route to the north-east blocked by the Ogwen glacier; it thereupon formed a large lake. Ever deepening, the lake eventually spilled over the high ground to the west and its waters not only joined those of Afon Braint but also scoured a channel through the 'barrier'. Thus, upon retreat of the glaciers and the consequent rise in sea level, the two-river system linked up, became a continuous waterway and Anglesey became an island.

The fault that gave rise to the waterway is known as the Dinorwig Fault. It lies beneath the Strait but also extends into Liverpool Bay and down the Llŷn Peninsula. The Dinorwig Fault and other faults south of Abermenai are active, as the residents of south-east Anglesey discovered when rudely awoken one

Ice magic

Plas Penrhyn dock

Sunday morning in July 1984 by a kind of roaring-sighing noise, followed immediately by a considerable shaking of the ground and buildings. The earthquake's epicentre was pinpointed in the Llŷn Penninsula. Its shock waves lasted for a minute or two and, while not very severe in Richter terms, its after-shocks persisted for several momths.

Today the scene appears a great deal more peaceful! Indeed, apart from otter footprints along the muddy tidal reaches of Afon Braint and a family of swans, river life seems to be scarce and it may be something of a relief to the eye when the Stepping Stones come into view, providing walkers with a safe river-crossing at any stage of the tide.

Before the motor car and metalled roads appeared, ordinary people in Anglesey had to travel on foot. Distance was therefore an important consideration and, for those living around Dwyran and Newborough, Caernarfon across the Strait was actually nearer than any Anglesey town. It was still a three-mile trek across the fields for Newborough folk to reach Tal-y-foel but then the ferry took them directly into Caernarfon. The only problem was the tidal river, Afon Braint, which crossed their path; easily fordable around low water but about three feet deep at high water. Under the circumstances, a boat would not have helped and a bridge would have been a major undertaking. The Stepping Stones must have been an ideal solution; it isn't hard to imagine the local villagers homeward-bound after a day in Caernarfon, stepping carefully from stone to stone above the waters of the river with their shopping bags and parcels.

There are twenty-eight massive limestone blocks crossing the river in a line, each weighing perhaps three tons. Who knows which forgotten hero sourced the limestone, quarried the blocks, transported them and then lifted them into position? Although not quite on the same scale as Telford's crossing of the Menai, this was no mean achievement.

After the Stepping Stones, a long straight lane leads back to the A4080, to a point less than a mile from Newborough. A left turn along the main road brings this stage of the walk to a close at the roundabout.

Taking the long view

Afon Braint stepping stones

III From Newborough to Bodorgan

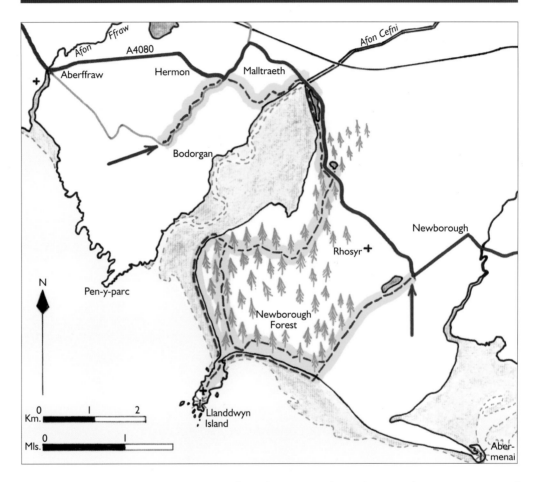

In which we meet wind-blown and seaborne sand at this southern extremity of Anglesey. We walk among impressive dunes, along two pristine beaches and skirt the sand-filled estuary of Afon Cefni. We hear about long-gone crafts, coal mining and an early Telford visit but our lasting memory is certain to be of Llanddwyn Island, a truly magical place.

Gafrod (marram stooks) sculpture

Sand-dune

Sea holly

Although Newborough appears in the title of this stage and is visible on the hill half a mile from the A4080 roundabout, the coastal route actually avoids the village altogether. But such is its historical importance to the area that it would be wrong to pass Newborough by without a mention.

It was a team of archaeologists in 1996 that brought the early history of Newborough back into focus when their excavations revealed a large hall and other buildings of the Llys or Royal Court at Rhosyr, (Newborough), which had lain buried in the sand for the best part of seven hundred years. Rhosyr was one of five royal estates in medieval Anglesey, each with a 'llys' at its heart, where the Princes of Gwynedd would stay during their travels around the kingdom dealing with local administration and legal disputes.

It is known that Llywelyn the Great issued a charter from Rhosyr in 1237 and that in 1283, English King Edward I also stayed there. Conjecturally, this visit could have sown a seed in Edward's mind, for when he launched his last and most ambitious castle and borough building programme near Llan-faes eight years later, he cleared the area where his *Beau Marais* castle and town were to be built, relocating the displaced population to a site adjacent to Rhosyr which he called Newborough. It received its Royal Charter in 1303.

The route commences south-westward, along a straight and narrow lane, passing a few houses, on the way down to a car park where there is an unexpected modern sculpture in steel, painted bright yellow. The sculpture tells a story for it represents the stooks of marram grass or gafrod, a simple but essential plant in this region. The five or six square miles of sand-dunes comprising Newborough's Warren and Forest not only give the area its special character but also, because of the instability of the dunes, a cause for concern. Severe storms can destroy the dunes and bury local farmland at the same time and it was such an event that obliterated the old Llys at Rhosyr seven hundred years ago. The roots of marram grass help to stabilise the dunes and local residents saw it to be in their interest to ask Elizabeth I to ensure that the marram grass was legally protected!

Adjacent to the car park is Llyn Rhos-ddu, a small lake favoured by many species of water bird that can be viewed from a nearby hide. Down towards the beach in Llanddwyn Bay to the east spreads a wide-open area of sand-dunes stretching into the distance and it is easy to see why it is known as the Warren! Before myxomatosis took its toll in the 1950s, the annual rabbit catch here was reputed to be in the order of 100,000. The area also boasts its own ecosystem with delightful displays in miniature of wild flowers and fungi amid the wind-sculpted dunes, some reaching thirty feet in height. There is an abundance of marram grass which, in the past, also supported a cottage industry in Newborough where the dried marram was woven into baskets, mats, ropes and the like. To the west, the dunes provide a home for today's cash crop in the shape of a forest of Corsican pine, a species of tree chosen for the dune-setting capabilities of its root system.

Just before reaching the beach, the coastal path turns north-westward through the forest, presumably to provide a safe route at all states of the tide and weather but, if possible, the dune-backed beach is a must. Dropping down onto the beach, the visitor's first impression is of a huge expanse of pristine sand, sculpted by wind and tide; then stunning views in the sweep of Traeth Llanddwyn towards Abermenai in the east and Llanddwyn Island in the west; then across Caernarfon Bay with breakers on its sand-bar,

Traeth Llanddwyn

to the very distinctive range of hills on the Llŷn, known as Yr Eifl. Walkers linger here for clearly this is a special place.

The highlight of this stage has to be Llanddwyn Island. For most of the time Llanddwyn is merely a promontory, projecting almost a mile into Caernarfon Bay; it becomes an 'island' for a short period only over high water on spring tides. Geologically, much of the island is volcanic in origin although the eruptions took place beneath the sea. Among the rocks at Llanddwyn, geologists have identified pillow lavas of a type of basalt known as spilite, which originally erupted onto an ancient ocean floor over 550 million years ago. Some well-defined pillows can still be found while others are much distorted and chemically transformed through contact with the sediments into which the lava was expelled; and the sediments, now

metamorphosed, exist as strikingly pink-and-cream-coloured rocks at the southern end of the island. The shoreline, often dark and jagged rock with off-lying islets, protects a number of small beaches and sand-filled coves, a joy for the boating fraternity. There are lovely places for picnicking and the area is visited daily by numerous walkers who come to view the birdlife and delicate flora of this beautiful nature reserve. Walkers may also find that their progress is being watched by the occasional seal!

In addition to the ancient rocks and physical attractions of the island, its human history and legend also go back a long way, to the fifth century when Dwynwen, unable to marry her Prince Maelon, chose to devote herself to God's service for the rest of her life. Broken-hearted herself, her aim was to help meet the hopes and dreams of all true lovers who came to her church and to her well upon the island. Thus she became the Welsh patron saint of lovers. The Latin cross near the big lighthouse was erected to her memory in 1897 and records her supposed death as 25 January, AD 465. Legend has it that, beside her well, there was a rock which was magically split in two to allow the dying Dwynwen to sit in comfort while she watched her last sunset . . . The church ruins nearby are all that remain of Saint Dwynwen's church of the sixteenth century, from which the island took its 'Llanddwyn' name. An adjacent Celtic cross commemorates three poor souls who were buried on the island. Their names are not revealed but in translation the Welsh inscription reads:

> 'Here we three lie at our journey's end,
> peacefully in the corner of a field,
> where you will be certain to follow.'

The picturesque row of tiny white cottages was built for the pilots who were stationed at Llanddwyn and whose job it was to guide vessels through the shifting sandbanks on the bar and onward to Caernarfon.

Pillow lava

Dwynwen's last sunset

Charles Tunnicliffe at Newborough

'From Newborough village a lane winds southwards and as it passes the old hilltop church there are wonderful views of the straits and the mainland mountains which fill the eastern and southern prospects. Past a few little stone farms it winds and then, dropping to the level of the dunes, the lane becomes a cart-track and then a path which, with difficulty, fights for its existence against the wind-driven sand of the dunes. Over hillocks of sand and marram grass and across flat pans, some of which still held considerable pools, we made our way until, at last, we came to the shore and the narrow causeway which connects the island of Llanddwyn to Anglesey.'

C. F. Tunnicliffe, *Shorelands Summer Diary*

CHARLES TUNNICLIFFE

✤ Born in 1901 in Langley, Cheshire

✤ Won a scholarship to the Royal College of Art in London

✤ Moved to Anglesey in 1947, to Shorelands, a cottage on Afon Cefni estuary

✤ Specialised in depicting wildlife, especially birds in natural settings

✤ Between 1957 and 1965 illustrated for Brooke Bond tea cards

✤ Work was widely seen in the 1960s through illustrations for Ladybird Books

✤ Illustrated 'Tarka the Otter' by Henry Williamson

✤ Died in 1979, leaving bequest to Anglesey Council

✤ Tunnicliffe collection housed at Oriel Ynys Môn, Llangefni

Celtic cross

Ponies at Llanddwyn

Celandines

The Llanddwyn pilots also maintained the light in the large white tower. Unusually, but because of the height of the promontory upon which the tower was built, a sufficient range of navigational light was achieved from a lantern room constructed at the base of the tower rather than at its top. Today, however, a solar-powered automatic light shines out from the smaller tower nearby. Tedium was unlikely to be a problem for the pilots as they also organised the lifeboat that was established there in 1840. If they observed a vessel in distress, they would summon the lifeboat crew by firing the cannons that stand in front of the cottages. Alas, road and rail communications superseded commercial shipping in these parts and the pilots moved on, perhaps rather sorry to leave their tiny cottages and their wonderful

view of the three peaks of Yr Eifl on the Llŷn Peninsula.

It is always sad to leave the romance and mystique of Llanddwyn Island. Heading north-westwards into Malltraeth Bay, the walker again faces a choice of route: to tread the sands of Traeth Penrhos which skirt the dunes and woodland, or take the shorter route through the forest itself to regain the A4080. Tide permitting, the beach route generates a feeling of immense space but progress through the soft sand, pebbles and seashells can be slow. After rejoining the peaceful forest track, birdwatchers need to look out for the ravens that have recently set up home here.

Immediately, on the opposite side of the main road, hidden in the trees, is a small lake with a permanent coot and moorhen population augmented by passing ducks and geese. There are two bird-hides for those who wish to dally. The route continues north-westwards but this time atop the mile-long Malltraeth Cob, an embankment built by the young engineer Thomas Telford at the end of the eighteenth century to prevent flooding of the Malltraeth Marsh by the sea, thereby reclaiming valuable farmland. (Previously, at high tide, the marsh flooded as far as Llangefni.) The present arrangements provide a man-made triple waterway comprising a central main channel for Afon Cefni, a tidal river, flanked by two lesser channels to carry away drainage from the marsh. All three channels are controlled by storm

gates at Malltraeth bridge. A distant viaduct crosses the marsh and its three channels, providing a fleeting glimpse of the London to Holyhead railway.

Built upon a narrow band of Millstone Grit, the name given to a sequence of sedimentary rocks found in coal-mining areas, the village of Malltraeth is quite small, with little evidence remaining to show that in the eighteenth and nineteenth centuries there was considerable mining activity in Malltraeth Marsh. The Parys Mountain copper mines were the main customers for fuel from Malltraeth's pits, the coal being transported overland by horse and cart or carried down-river to the sea in barges, bound for Amlwch and other destinations. And as in so many of Anglesey's coastal villages, shipbuilding was an essential industry here too. There are two public houses on the village main street, each reckoned to be at least two hundred years old; old enough to have fed and watered the long-gone shipbuilders and miners of Malltraeth.

Today the village is mainly residential and has about a mile of interesting dwellings lining the western shore of the estuary, from whose windows residents can watch glorious sunrises over the distant mountains, with the light shafting down over Newborough Forest and the vast sands of Malltraeth. In years gone by, one notable resident was the very popular artist Charles Tunnicliffe, whose particular talent was exceptional draughtsmanship and meticulous studies of birds visiting the Cefni estuary.

The route leads south-westwards from the village centre, along several lanes and footpaths, around houses and gardens, until it turns to the north-west and climbs a narrow metalled road up to the crossroads. Turning left here, the trail takes the lesser road south-westwards. For about a mile, this road follows the high Bodorgan estate wall. Neat little 'windows' have been built into this wall, enabling walkers to look in upon the grazing livestock although this was not likely to have been their original purpose: there are pheasants everywhere! After passing a couple of estate gatehouses, the road turns sharply to the right, away from the estate; a good point at which to terminate the third stage of the walk.

Telford's Cob

Cottage at Malltraeth

IV From Bodorgan to Rhosneigr

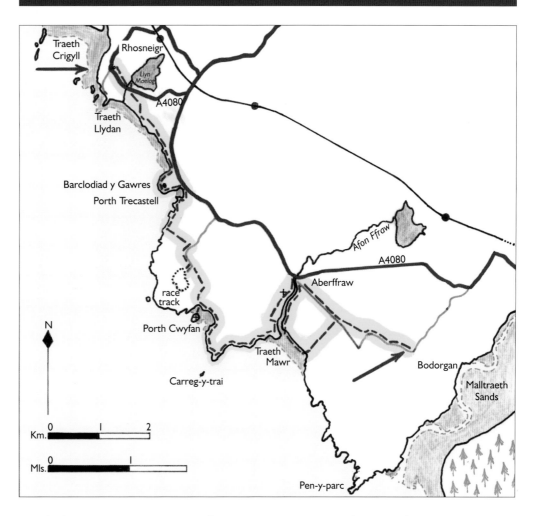

In which we experience a stage of immense contrasts: in the east, charming enigmatic Aberffraw with its incomparable history and its old packhorse bridge which carries us across Afon Ffraw into the village. Then in the west, we pass a race track and burial chamber before walking on to Rhosneigr, a resort that owes its being to the advent of the railway.

Ground willow

Houses at Aberffraw

Mouth of Afon Ffraw

The fourth stage of the walk 'All Around Anglesey' starts outside the Bodorgan estate where the little road heading south-west turns abruptly to lead west-north-west. It is a spot surrounded by wide-open green fields, mostly given over to sheep, with a farm or two and just a few dwellings dotted about. The underlying rock in these parts is Gwna green-schist, another of Anglesey's Precambrian metamorphic rocks and distinctly green in colour because of the presence of chlorite. It's only about 130 feet above sea level here and yet the view ahead, over the low-lying coastline, is uninterrupted, with a first sighting of Holyhead Mountain thirteen miles away. The route ahead mainly follows the narrow road, in a nearly straight line to the ancient village of Aberffraw, a mile and a half distant.

After a gentle descent to Tywyn Aberffraw, a square mile of sand-dunes extending almost to the village itself, there is a choice of route: along the road, straight across the dunes or, for those who love beaches, to the south-west along the dunes' edge, to Traeth Mawr at the head of Aberffraw Bay. This superb dune-backed beach and, further on, the estuary of Afon Ffraw, lead back to the delightful old packhorse bridge, erected in 1731, bearing those on foot over the river to the waterfront buildings of the village. It is pleasant to wander around Aberffraw which is peaceful and untroubled by the A4080. There is a village square with a few shops, cafés and pubs and any number of ways down to the river, suggesting that access to the sea for Aberffraw's shipbuilders, for transport and for trade, was of considerable importance in years gone by. St Beuno's church near the village centre may look rather sombre outwardly but it is most interesting and attractive within. Its twin aisles, divided by a light arcade, give it an open and cheerful feeling while the twelfth-century Norman carved arch behind the font may provide a tantalising link with Aberffraw's medieval glory.

It seems hardly credible that this peaceful little village on the west bank of Afon Ffraw was once the capital of north Wales, and even more astonishing that the precise location of its pre-eminent royal court has been lost in the mists of time. Yet, such enigmas are entirely in keeping with the charm and mystique of Aberffraw. Perhaps the Maes Llywelyn housing estate knows the answers?

Any of several pathways heading southwards from the village will lead down to the river mouth, surprisingly narrow and very shallow at low water. On a small rounded headland guarding the river entrance, known as Trwyn Du, both Stone Age and Bronze Age people left their mark. Apart from half a dozen stones protruding through the grass, there is little to see, but previous excavations have unearthed evidence of a hunting camp dating back to 7,000 BC and the visible stones are associated with a burial mound dating back to about 2,000 BC.

From here the coastal path trends south-westwards, just above extensive weed-covered rocks jutting seaward, until it rounds Braich-lwyd, a rocky headland with an off-lying reef called Carreg-y-trai; a good place for seal-spotting at low water with a good pair of binoculars. Having turned the corner, sharp-eyed walkers may be able to detect the transition from Gwna green-schist to silver-coloured mica schist in the shoreline rocks. In April and May there is a brilliant display of gorse and spring flowers. From Braich-lwyd the path leads northwards into an attractive bay encompassing both Porth Cwyfan and Porth China, two areas of beach separated by a built-up 'island' upon which Saint Cwyfan's church stands in splendid isolation. Known locally as the 'Church in the Sea', for the high tide surrounds it completely, it was founded

Packhorse bridge

back in the seventh century by Saint Cwyfan. The present building was erected five hundred years later although it is clear that the north aisle of the original twin-aisled design has since been removed. Enchanting on a calm sunny day, but storage of the church bell within the porch and some tough fibreglass windows are powerful reminders of the little church's extreme exposure to the elements; it is easy to imagine what might have befallen the north aisle. Two services are still held in the summer, depending upon tide and weather.

From Porth China a narrow road heads northwards and inland, skirting what used to be an MOD firing range but is now Anglesey's race-track for two and four-wheeled vehicles. Along the road, away from the race-track, a coastal path sign points north-westwards across fields to regain the coastline. Most of the fields in these parts are grazed by sheep but occasionally there are cattle, and a stampeding herd of inquisitive young heifers can be a considerable test of nerve for walkers.

Folded rocks near Ynys Lawd

Anglesey rocks

The author's model of Anglesey's geology.

All rocks fall into three basic groups: igneous, sedimentary and metamorphic; examples of all three are exposed along Anglesey's coastline.

Igneous rocks are formed by the crystallization of once-molten material known as 'magma' below and 'lava' above the surface. Llanddwyn Island's pillow lavas and the granite at Porth Nobla are good examples.

Sedimentary rocks are formed at the Earth's surface, mostly from sediments on the seabed. The limestones at Moelfre and Penmon consist mainly of once-living marine organisms while the dunes, beaches and sandbanks along the south-west shore of Anglesey, if undisturbed, are destined to become sandstone.

Metamorphic rocks are formed from the alteration of a pre-existing rock, either igneous or sedimentary, through such agencies as heat and pressure. Once mudstones, Anglesey's several schists are good examples: they resulted from their deep burial and folding within the Earth's crust.

Away from the coastline, much of Anglesey's bedrock is hidden beneath thick deposits of boulder clay left behind by ice-age ice sheets. If these deposits could be planed off and the flat rock surface then polished, the result might look something like the model in the photograph.

timewatch

700–545
million years ago

Rocks such as glaucophane schist and mica schist, quartzitic tuffs and metamorphosed sandstones and mudstones date from the Precambrian period. Striking bands of Gwna green-schist can be found in the island.

545–300
million years ago

The Palaeozoic is the era of the Cambrian rocks (probably completely absent from Anglesey), Ordovician shales, sandstones, conglomerates and ironstones, Silurian mudstones, Devonian Old Red Sandstones and Carboniferous Limestone. An outcrop of Devonian Old Red Sandstone contrasts colourfully with the neighbouring limestone at Lligwy Bay.

65
million years ago

The Cenozoic era saw the formation of dykes, cliffs of glacier debris and drumlins. Molten rock invaded much older Gwna green-schist to create this dyke at Gallows Point.

'MÔN MAM CYMRU'

It is Anglesey's rocks that have shaped the island's landscape and therefore its development; they affect the lives of everyone living here. Through erosion, the rocks influence the nature of the soil and thereby control the variety of crops and livestock that the land can support. It follows that the rocks made a fundamental contribution towards the island's early importance as a producer of grain and its former title 'Mother of Wales'. Direct exploitation of the rocks has been and still is of great importance to the island's economy. The mineral riches they contain have yielded copper and other valuable metals; mines once produced coal and quarries huge quantities of limestone and other building materials. In addition, the kilning of limestone was once a regular Anglesey practice, to release its calcium oxide as an early form of fertiliser for the land.

Rocks stained by iron oxides at Porth Saint

Anglesey's rocks are mainly of the Precambrian and Palaeozoic eras and are of great interest to geologists. Some of the Precambrian formations are world renowned and, together with the fossils, dykes and several intriguing rock features, it is easy to see why the island has become something of a 'mecca' for geologists.

The large inlet of Porth Trecastell, walled in on both sides by cliffs and rocks has a large and firm sandy beach at its head. The inlet is also remembered locally as Cable Bay as the first underwater telegraph cables once led from this point to Ireland and then onward across the Atlantic Ocean. With such easy access provided by the A4080 road, this is a popular location for water sports, beach activities and cliff-path walks. The alignment of Porth Trecastell leaves it exposed to the south-west and a good breeze or ocean swell from that quarter makes it a favourite with surfboarders. On such days, however, those who would rather build sandcastles may have to endure the stinging discomfort of wind-driven sand. From Trecastell car park, a good cliff path leads westward and upward along the north side of the inlet to a chambered grave known as Barclodiad y Gawres, on the headland. Dating back to about 2,500 BC, it was originally covered by a mound of earth and stones but, in the reconstruction, it has been given a roof of concrete and glass whose profile matches the terrain. Access is gained via a stone passage but the underground inner chambers are protected by locked iron gates. A key can be borrowed but there is just sufficient light, standing at the gates, to make out the large carved stones within.

If our Bronze Age forebears had time and leisure to pause, perhaps they turned their gaze seaward to watch the patches of reflected sunlight stealing across the water's pewter-coloured surface. The sea and sky are such important parts of each and every coastal view, but are so easily taken for granted. They apparently meet at the horizon, a mysterious and elusive line. For an observer at Barclodiad y Gawres, the horizon is about eight miles distant but, for someone at the water's edge, it is less than three miles away; so close, yet nobody has ever reached it! Time to move on.

Barclodiad y Gawres

Porth Trecastell

Descending from the headland in a north-eastward direction, the path leads to another inlet, Porth Nobla, similar to the previous inlet but on a lesser scale in all respects. Rock exposures on Porth Nobla's beach are of granite, marking the visible tip of an intrusive igneous mass of rock which lies in a mile-wide strip, ten miles in length, north-eastward across the island. From the head of this beach to the outskirts of Rhosneigr is a walk of just a mile, following either the well-trodden coastal path through the dunes and marram grass, or the firm sands of Traeth Llydan with its scattering of rocky outcrops. The dunes are populated mainly by rabbits but they also conceal a small caravan park and, unexpectedly, an isolated group of substantial dwellings with the Maelog Hotel nearby. At the point where the path converges with the A4080, just outside Rhosneigr, lies the shallow and heavily-reeded Llyn Maelog, noted for its birdlife. A small river from the east runs into the lake which, in turn, drains into the sea from its westernmost corner. The main road crosses this very short river via a concrete bridge but, alongside, the old bridge of stone still stands and looks as though it might have been designed by committee! Rhosneigr is surrounded by sand but the village itself stands upon a small area of beautifully folded Ordovician rock.

Until the 1870s, Rhosneigr was a tiny seaside village of scattered white cottages. Its inhabitants survived by catching lobsters for shipment to Liverpool and other markets. But its magnificent beaches, a nearby station on the newly-completed Holyhead railway and the Maelog Hotel all combined to attract summer visitors in large numbers. Many took root, building their own houses in and around the village, and soon Rhosneigr became an energetic holiday resort. Today the lobster fishing has all but gone. But, with its miles of safe sand afforded by Traeth Llydan and Traeth Crigyll, there are boundless opportunities for holiday-makers with young families. The dune-backed beaches are also grand for walking, while the rock-pools of the large Cerrig-y-brain outcrop harbour a range of interesting marine life for those who like to explore. The resort has also become a popular centre for water sports. The A4080 leads directly into the village to the war memorial clock at the crossroads which brings the fourth stage of the walk to a close.

Towards Rhosneigr

Fishermen at Barclodiad y Gawres

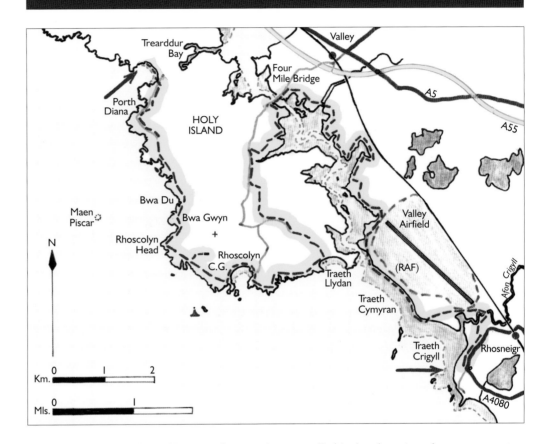

In which we visit the Valley aerodrome, the so-called 'Inland Sea' and some amazing geology on Holy Island. We cross the old Four Mile Bridge, see some beautiful bays and find traces of the island's once prized Green Marble. We hear about gangs of wreckers and how an act of instinctive loyalty cost one brave dog its life.

A rocky cleft

Rhosneigr's war memorial clock

Ruined cottages at the 'Inland Sea'

Leaving Rhosneigr's war memorial behind and proceeding clockwise along the A4080 circuit for about half a mile, the route then turns north-west into Warren Road, bears right and drops down to a wooden footbridge over Afon Crigyll. This small meandering river, back in the eighteenth century, was the haunt of a notorious gang of ship-wreckers whose aim was to lure passing ships into danger and then to help themselves to the cargoes and the vessels' fittings. Eventually the wreckers were caught, tried at Beaumaris and it was expected that they would hang. But the story goes that the judge was in such a state of intoxication that, instead of passing sentence, he ordered the wreckers to be released!

Ahead lie some two square miles of open peaty marshland known as Tywyn Trewan. Since 1941, much of this area has been taken up by the several runways and hangars of Valley airfield. During the later war years, Valley was strategically important for the transatlantic flights of the US Air Force. Since then, however, it has been 'home' to the Nineteenth and Twenty-second Squadrons of the RAF whose respective roles include advanced training for jet aircraft pilots, and search and rescue duties. Inhabitants of north-west Wales are much aware of both of these functions. Two-seater Hawk trainers, disturbing the peace as they streak across the sky, can be tiresome, but the invaluable service provided by the helicopters in rescuing seafarers, mountain walkers and other distressed souls more than compensates for any disturbance. The footpath westward through the dunes skirts the airfield but, as is the case along much of this coastline, walkers have the option of the beach if the tide allows. In this case, Traeth Crigyll and Traeth Cymyran which meet at Ynys Feurig, provide mainly firm sand and probably the quickest route to the entrance to the 'Inland Sea', that three-mile-long stretch of water lying between mainland Anglesey and Ynys Gybi or Holy Island.

The southern entrance to the 'Inland Sea' is quite narrow, with strong tidal streams, but it is clearly marked by the attractive white-painted dwellings at Plas Cymyran. From this point, a well-worn track leads north-eastwards to link up with the end of the Llanfair-yn-neubwll road, right under the airfield's main flight path. This is an exciting and very popular location from which to observe the jet aircraft taking off and landing. The airfield's main buildings and control tower lie between the runways and the railway while the MOD's accommodation for Service personnel fringes the road to Llanfihangel-yn-Nhywyn. Llyn Cerrig Bach is one of several small shallow lakes in this area and while airfield contractors were digging out peat from around the lake to stabilise dunes adjacent to the runways, they discovered a large hoard of Iron Age weapons and other artefacts. This most important find of bronze and iron objects is now displayed at the National Museum of Wales in Cardiff. What would the Iron Age spear-carrying warrior make of today's missile-carrying jet fighter travelling faster than sound?

The coastal path up the eastern side of the 'Inland Sea' to Four Mile Bridge is about twice as far as the proverbial crow would fly. With arable and grazing land to the east and the 'Inland Sea' to the west, it is a gentle but convoluted walk with an abundance of gorse, picturesque and pleasant on a sunny day. An occasional stone-built farm comes into view and several dwellings overlook the waterway and its inlets, although extensive sand and mud flats appear at low tide when 'Inland Trickle' might be a more appropriate name than 'Inland Sea'.

Before Telford built the Stanley Embankment, Four Mile Bridge was the only means of access to Holy Island and Holyhead, other than by boat. The bridge takes its name from being exactly four miles from Holyhead, via the B4545, and is more of a stone wall than a bridge, although there is a single small arch at its mid-length. Built in 1675, there is a hint in its Welsh name, 'Pontrhypont', that a low-tide ford

Hawk trainers at RAF Valley

pre-dated the bridge. Well-established housing and a few interesting shops cluster around the bridge, then a few yards beyond its western end there is a small terrace of charming little cottages.

The coastal path leaves the road here and immediately heads south from the end of the bridge parapet along the muddy-grassy western shore of the 'Inland Sea'. Walkers need to be wary of the lush green tufty grass as it is practically afloat in places! Low stone walls and outcrops of green mica schist here are interesting for the variety and profusion of lichens they carry. About half a mile from the bridge, the path turns south-westwards, away from the shore, through narrow hedged lanes and then up to attractive white farm buildings at Rhyd-y-bont. Wild flowers abound and a well-made track of hard-packed rubble leads down to join the Rhoscolyn road.

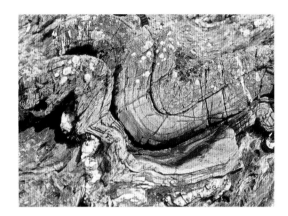

If examined closely, the rubble reveals fragments of a pale green rock, speckled with black. This is because the track crosses a small and rare deposit of serpentinite, a rock that can be cut, turned and polished as ornamental material. Now effectively worked out, this valuable rock used to be known as Mona Green Marble and was included in the building of Bristol, Peterborough and Worcester cathedrals.

Half a mile due south along the Rhoscolyn road, the coastal path leaves the road to the east and heads into a rather boggy area planted recently with alder, hazel and rowan. The path climbs a shoulder to join the narrow road leading down to Traeth Llydan (Silver Bay) and in springtime the woodland is carpeted with bluebells. The 'Inland Sea' comes into view again as the narrow Traeth Llydan road, trending south-eastwards, crosses an area of level and productive-looking farmland; a typical Anglesey scene, in fact, with a few farms and houses dotted about, some of the buildings looking rather forlorn. The road dwindles to a pathway and gently descends to a neat coppice of Corsican pine where a carefully fenced track through the trees delivers walkers abruptly to Silver Bay, at the south-east corner of Holy Island.

Silver Bay must come close to any definition of a perfect beach for holiday-makers. Its dune-backed pristine sand lies in a flawless arc, bounded east and west by low rocky headlands. It faces south, looking into Cymyran Bay, with Rhosneigr in the distance. It is safe for bathers and yet the beach shelves sufficiently to allow small craft close inshore. Despite the proximity of the airfield, the disturbance is minimal, as the flight-path is almost a mile away. Only the weather could spoil such an idyllic situation.

The route westward along the cropped grass of the cliff-top path to Borth-wen and Rhoscolyn makes for easy walking, and yet the nearby cliffs are steep, broken and deeply cleft by the action of the sea. The rock is green mica schist, greenish in colour and remarkable in appearance, for its severe distortions are evidence of the immense forces involved in the massive movements of the Earth's crust that once affected this part of Anglesey. Wild flowers are everywhere, tucked into rock crevices and growing in the open heath. Over the cliff edge at low tide, long streamers of golden-brown kelp stir lazily in the swell, and rock-pools show off colourful weed, shellfish and anemones.

Folded rocks

Long strands of kelp

A Bay in Anglesey

The sleepy sound of a tea-time tide
Slaps at the rocks the sun has dried.

Too lazy, almost, to sink and lift
Round low peninsulas pink with thrift.

The water, enlarging shells and sand,
Grows greener emerald out from land

And brown over shadowy shelves below
The waving forests of seaweed show.

. . .

And filling in, brimming in, sparkling
and free
The sweet susurration of incoming sea.

John Betjeman

JOHN BETJEMAN

✠ Born on 28 August, 1906, near Highgate, London

✠ Attended Marlborough College and Magdalen College, Oxford

✠ Taught briefly and in 1930 joined 'The Architectural Review' as assistant editor

✠ Published first book of poems in 1931

✠ Became film critic on the 'Evening Standard'

✠ With John Piper edited Shell Guides to the counties of Britain: 'North Wales: Caernarvonshire, Anglesey, Denbighshire and Flintshire' appeared in 1971

✠ Pursued a prolific writing and broadcasting career

✠ Documentaries: 'Metroland' and 'A Passion for Churches'

✠ Became Poet Laureate in 1972

✠ Died in 1984 at his home in Trebetherick, Cornwall

'Tyger'

Pink campion

Wall of many colours

Marked by the Rhoscolyn Beacon to seaward, the extensive inlet of Borth-wen provides safe and sheltered moorings for mariners who know where the reefs are, and an attractive stretch of water leading to a good sandy beach at its head. The buildings are mostly private homes, painted white, and scattered rather than clustered. The old lifeboat station and slipway still attract attention, as do the raucous sea birds nesting on Ynys Traws.

Silver Bay and Rhoscolyn are both popular, yet unspoiled, seaside destinations for holiday-makers and visitors on warm sunny days. There are also caravan parks but they are not obtrusive, and access to both beaches is restricted to single-track roads which zigzag their way down to the shore. China clay was once quarried in these parts but no industry is

evident today. Rhoscolyn's conspicuous church was founded by Saint Gwenfaen in the sixth century and her holy well, just half a mile west of the church, is reputed to have certain healing properties although the mere prospect of 'taking the waters' from this well would surely cure most ailments!

Leaving Borth-wen behind, the path again follows the configurations of the coast although, this time, above even higher cliffs. The climb up to a disused coastguard lookout now 'manned' only by sheep gives good views out to Rhoscolyn Beacon and way back to Rhosneigr. Nearby is a four-sided stone seat built for Lady Margaret Verney so that she could enjoy the incomparable views yet remain sheltered from the wind, whatever its direction. From this superb vantage point, the whole coastline is visible from Borth-wen to Bwa Du, completely embracing the extraordinary Precambrian schistose and quartzose rock formations of south-west Holy Island. Just before the gentle descent towards Rhoscolyn Head, there is a slate memorial to Professor Dennis Wood (1934-2001), a well-known geologist who devoted most of his life to the study and interpretation of Anglesey's rocks.

Rhoscolyn Head's sheer hundred-foot cliff, mainly quartzite and plunging straight into the sea, is ample warning that any exploration of the rocks in this area demands the utmost caution. This is a region of complex rock-folding resulting from impact between two of the Earth's crustal plates. 550 million years ago, give or take a year or two, sand and mud were deposited beneath the sea in this region and gradually consolidated into sandstone and mudstone which, in turn, slowly transformed into the quartzites and schists seen today. Later interaction between the Earth's crustal plates formed a large-scale up-fold or anticline before it was buckled and squeezed into the highly folded and distorted rocks evident in today's cliffs.

The path now leads north-westwards, past St Gwenfaen's Well, over the top of Rhoscolyn Head and then north-eastwards, following an unusual and attractive high stone wall; the mason was undoubtedly artistic. The gentle descent into Porth Saint offers a feast of colour: white quartzite in the western part of the bay, then sandstone stained orange-brown by iron oxides and one conspicuous patch of pink haematite-rich rock in a cliff face of quartzite.

The path around the perimeter of Porth Saint gives onto a wide-open grassy plateau on its way to Bwa Gwyn, a natural and spectacular white arch developed along a fault zone in the quartzite. Then, halfway between Bwa Gwyn and Bwa Du, a second natural arch but black this time, there is a simple headstone marking an act of instinctive loyalty:

TYGER Sep. 17th 1819.

Exactly one mile due west from the headstone lies an off-shore rock called Maen Piscar, visible at low water but not at other stages of the tide, and the story goes that a Liverpool-bound ketch struck the rock in thick fog and subsequently sank. This put the master, two

Rhoscolyn Head

men and a boy in a fearful predicament for not only were they left in the water but, because of the fog, they had no idea of the direction in which to swim to safety. It seemed they were doomed except that the master's pet dog, Tyger, appeared to know instinctively where the land was and began to swim in that direction, with the boy holding onto his collar. All were totally exhausted on reaching land and the dog helped drag the men ashore. Thus the crew survived but, sadly, not Tyger, who quietly died from his exertions.

Bwa Du marks the northern limit of the Rhoscolyn anticline. In fact, a well-exposed geological fault runs north-westward through this location, part of the continuous fault which can be traced from Borth-wen to North Stack, and is easily identified by the gully between the yellowish quartzite to the south-

west and the green mica schist to the north-east. From here, the route heads north-north-west up the coast, with rugged cliff scenery interrupted occasionally by small inlets and bays, particularly Porth-y-garan. The coastal path passes right through a caravan park just before linking up with a service road from Trearddur. Along the road are many modern white houses and bungalows, some lived in and some 'weekend only', some befitting the environment and some, perhaps, a little out of place. North of Ravenspoint, however, there are two delightful little bays, Porth Castell and Porth Diana, together with properties more traditional in style.

With no particular coastal-path landmark at which to terminate this stage, the promenade above the sands of Trearddur Bay is an appropriate stopping place. After all, it would have been the beautiful bay that attracted Iarddur to these parts in the first place and, connected as it is with one of noble birth, it is not surprising that this famous Anglesey resort acquired the name: *Tre Iarddur*.

Bwa Gwyn

Porth Diana

VI From Trearddur Bay to the Stanley Embankment

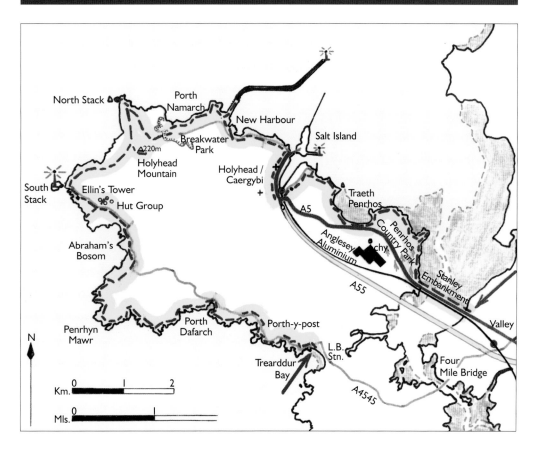

In which we admire Trinity House architecture, an Iron Age settlement, the Roman–wall remains of Caer Gybi, an enormous breakwater and the industrial and maritime splendours of Holyhead. We keep company with the rocky magnificence and spectacular birdlife along the coastal path and visit two splendid country parks.

Coastal scenery

A Welsh llama silhouetted against Holyhead Mountain

Porth Dafarch at low tide

As a seascape, Trearddur Bay is beautiful and it is not difficult to see why it has become so popular as a holiday resort and a dormitory area for Caergybi (Holyhead). Indeed, as a settlement, it dwarfs all others on this coast of Anglesey. But the coastal path does not encourage any pause for reconnoitre; instead, it cuts directly across the head of the bay and turns westward at the lifeboat station, following the road that leads eventually to South Stack.

In the first mile to Porth-y-post, the route passes Craig-y-môr, a dark and distinctive family home perched upon a headland in the bay, built entirely from stone shipped from Scotland. West of Porth-y-post, the path changes from roadside pavement and becomes a cliff-top walk again. It is increasingly dramatic, with cliffs estimated to be seventy or eighty

feet above the sea and penetrated by inlets, ravines and fissures of breathtaking proportions. Only Porth Dafarch, easily accessed from the road, offers a good, wide and attractive beach. Other inlets are rock strewn, severe and for the most part inaccessible, with striking quartzite rock formations and a massive dark-coloured igneous dyke cutting through the cliff and disappearing under water.

Two hundred years ago, before the Holyhead breakwater was built, Porth Dafarch was sometimes used by the Irish packets, in strong northerly winds, as a sheltered alternative to Holyhead. Even so, exceptional seamanship would have been required under sail to negotiate the bay, safely land and pick up the passengers. The path now skirts around Porth Ruffydd and crosses a large expanse of open land, gently losing height down to the heather and gorse-covered headland of Penrhyn Mawr. At this point, it turns northward to give a first view of South Stack lighthouse, two miles distant.

Amid heathland flowers, heather and gorse, across pale green-grey outcrops of quartzite, the path follows the cliffs over level terrain. There are striking views of South Stack and Ellin's Tower and, finally, the impressive rock wall of Abraham's Bosom. After a short distance along this north-eastward leg, a new section leads across green fields and back to the winding road. The walk uphill to South Stack is a pleasant one with roadside wild flowers, honeysuckle, exotic caterpillars and even a field of llamas for company. The route is marked by scattered white cottages and farms, with the bare, silver-grey mound of Mynydd Twr (Holyhead Mountain) above, almost glistening in the sunlight.

About a quarter mile before the end of the road there is an RSPB car park, giving access to Ellin's Tower. Directly opposite the car park entrance is a pathway leading up to what are known locally as Cytiau'r Gwyddelod (Irishmen's Huts), the site of an Iron Age settlement.

Along the footpath from below the RSPB car park, towards Ellin's Tower, a peep over the cliff edge can be quite frightening for the cliff-tops here must be two or three hundred feet above the sea. The reward, however, is a majestic view of the vertical wall of folded rock strata, consisting of alternating sandstone and mudstone beds, leading up to Ynys Lawd upon which South Stack lighthouse stands. In keeping with the scale of the scenery, a huge dyke of black igneous rock is also to be seen, parallel to the cliff face. Ellin's Tower itself was built in 1876 by the Hon W O Stanley of Penrhos (near Holyhead), for his wife Ellin and their family, from which to observe the myriads of seabirds wheeling around South Stack. For fifty years or more, the tower was a popular attraction but fell into disrepair after the Second World War. In 1980 the RSPB acquired the building and, after two years of restoration work, reopened it to the public as a birdlife information centre and observation point.

Access to the lighthouse is gained via a steep, stepped path that zigzags down the cliff face – 409 steps in all – to a metal bridge spanning the gap to Ynys Lawd. Mere words scarcely describe a visit to the

stack with its massive cliff faces of hugely folded strata, great chasms in the rocks and waves breaking far below; the sheer scale is unnerving. In May/June, hundreds of guillemot and razorbill precariously crowd onto narrow ledges in the cliff, to rear their young. First impressions after climbing down the cliff face and crossing the bridge are of white walls and white buildings surmounted by the tall white lighthouse standing before a fantastic wall of rock. The famous light emits a white flash every ten seconds and has a range of twenty-four miles; and on misty days, a nautophone emits a powerful three-second fog signal every thirty seconds. Diesel generators and keepers' quarters can still be seen but, in line with modern practice, South Stack lighthouse is now fully automatic and remotely-controlled though personnel are on hand to give visitors an informative guided tour.

Lesser black-backed gull and chick

Seabirds nesting on rock ledges

South Stack lighthouse

Back up the 409 steps to the road and to the coastal path which then trends generally north-eastward towards North Stack, skirting Gogarth Bay. Care is required as, in several places, the terrain falls away sharply to the sea. As a detour, it may be decided to scale Holyhead Mountain (Mynydd Twr) to look at the remains of the large defensive Iron Age hillfort of Caer y Twr. Stone ramparts encircle the summit and enclose some seventeen acres. From the top – where the Romans once had a watchtower – there is a panoramic view of Holyhead and its harbour. Back on the path, an enclosure fences off a number of dish-shaped transmitter aerials facing westward; these are microwave links with Ireland. Silhouetted against the silvery rock terrain, the effect is somewhat 'Martian'.

Rugged footpaths criss-cross the landscape between South and North Stack, some apparently disappearing into space at the cliff edges, but it is not difficult to pick a safe route. The layout of the premises at North Stack, once a fog signal station, now privately owned, shows the influence of Trinity House. Although only two miles from Holyhead, North Stack is a barren, windswept and lonely location with only seabirds, cliff-climbers, adders and the occasional photographer for company.

The eastward track towards Holyhead climbs initially and then descends quite rapidly in the vicinity of Porth Namarch, down to a levelled area known as 'Breakwater Country Park'. The Park, which opened in 1995, occupies the bed of an immense quarry that owes its existence to the construction of a huge breakwater, completed in 1873 and about one and a half miles in length, protecting Holyhead harbour from the prevailing south-westerlies. It was an incredible undertaking, involving over 1,300 men who, in the course of twenty-eight years, quarried nearly 7,000,000 tons of quartzite rock from the north-eastern flank of Holyhead Mountain, transported it by rail and then tipped it onto the seabed to form a massive foundation for the breakwater itself. Today, the sheer rock walls left by the quarrymen form the perimeter and backdrop to the Park which includes several small ponds, a delightful little lake, well-kept walks, a restored brickworks and archaeological displays.

Microwave communication with Ireland, Holyhead Mountain

Lake at Breakwater Country Park

Anglesey's lighthouses

It is sobering to imagine the problems in navigating a commercial sailing vessel around the coasts of Anglesey before there were any lighthouses, for these are treacherous waters indeed. The northern and western coastlines are mostly of solid rock, with many submerged reefs and isolated rocks lying offshore. Prevailing westerly winds frequently reach gale and sometimes storm force, making Anglesey a dangerous 'lee shore' for sailing vessels. Even on quieter days, sea fog is a possibility and early navigational equipment was limited to magnetic compass, log and leadline only.

In addition, Anglesey offers yet another hazard: the tidal streams. These can run up to five knots at times off the west and north coasts and could quickly lead a sailing vessel into danger. The perils were well recognised, not least by the people who lived on the island, and it was William Trench who set out to build the first Anglesey lighthouse on the Skerries, starting around 1716. By the mid-nineteenth century, lighthouses had been built at Llanddwyn, South Stack, Holyhead Breakwater, the Skerries, Point Lynas and Trwyn Du at Penmon although, of these, the most important for ships passing by Anglesey were those at South Stack, the Skerries and Point Lynas.

Early lighthouses were often little more than towers on top of which blazed a coal fire. Transporting the coal – often in difficult weather – was a feat of human endurance in itself although the power to collect fees from passing vessels seems to have made it all worthwhile.

Since 1836 Trinity House has been responsible for all UK lighthouses, an enabling Act allowing it to purchase all privately-owned establishments. Owners of the Skerries lighthouse, however, opposed the move, holding out for a purchase price of nearly half a million pounds.

1645

A petition to King Charles II to build the South Stack lighthouse was inexplicably refused.

1809

The paraffin oil lamps in the South Stack lantern were lit for the first time. The original tower 91 feet high was built upon the summit of Ynys Lawd.

1874

The height of the tower was raised to 197 feet above high water and a new lantern was fitted, increasing the range of the light.

1938

Following electrification in 1938, an almost frictionless bearing for the rotating five-ton lantern, guided by rollers, was introduced by floating the lantern upon a circular trough of mercury.

BELLS, GUNS AND OTHER SIGNALS

Fog signalling devices have certainly kept pace with advances in technology: the first fog signals from South Stack involved striking an inverted bell weighing two and a half tons; this was later replaced by a compressed-air horn emitting a mournful blast, in its turn to be replaced by an electric nautophone.

Before the building of the lighthouse at South Stack, the North Stack fog signal was important to ships making a landfall at Holyhead in poor visibility. There is a 'magazine' building at North Stack, as audible warnings to shipping were signalled by cannon fire. Presumably they fired blanks! The ex-naval cannon, a fearsome-looking weapon, is now mounted beside the coastal path. The cannon could be heard at distances up to about ten miles. There was also an unusual experimental underwater bell whose warning signal could be detected in an iron ship's hull up to a distance of about a mile.

Signalling systems were also used to communicate less dramatic but important information. Before the days of the electric telegraph, a unique semaphore system was set up to link Holyhead with Liverpool. This involved eleven signal stations spaced at approximately ten-mile intervals, each one having two tall signal masts and trained signalmen who could alert a Liverpool shipowner, in just five minutes, to a sighting of his ship off Holyhead and her expected time of arrival in Liverpool. Maintaining a constant lookout during daylight hours, the signalmen handled about 2,000 inward and outward reports each year.

Rocky Coast window

The Irish ferry passing North Stack

Lord Stanley's fortification of Holyhead Harbour in response to the threat of French invasion during the Napoleonic wars

The Rocky Coast, eastward from Porth Namarch, offers a few small caves and interesting rock-pools but is difficult to negotiate on foot; much safer to view it from the recognised path that eventually leads down to Soldiers Point and the root of the breakwater. Understandably, the coastal path does not include the breakwater itself but, under the right conditions, it is tempting to walk out to the square-shaped lighthouse at its seaward end, where there is a good view of inward- and outward-bound ferries. Walking the breakwater takes about an hour and a half and offers a prospect of Holyhead's New Harbour, together with a closer look at the special berth serving Anglesey Aluminium and a view across Holyhead Bay towards Carmel Head and the Skerries. The breakwater truly is a feat of civil engineering

which provided much-needed shelter for the Dublin packet boats and other commercial vessels using the port; it also secured a future for Holyhead.

It was the breakwater's contractor who built Soldiers Point for himself and his family. His distinguished-looking house, more recently a hotel, boasts a grand castellated design with high garden walls to match. From Soldiers Point, the route south-eastwards into Holyhead follows Newry Beach Road and Prince of Wales Road (which together make up the promenade), passing Trinity Marina, the Lifeboat Station and Sailing Club, the Maritime Museum and the Coastguard Station, before reaching the Old Harbour area. There is no access for the general public to Salt Island and the Dublin ferry terminal but beyond the security fence there are several interesting-looking buildings within the port area, in particular, the Custom or Clock House, Port Control, and the Admiralty Arch leading to the Mail Pier (which was the very first Irish packet berth). At the time of its construction to commemorate King George IV's visit, Admiralty Arch stood beside the railway that used to run out to Salt Island and it also marked the end of the A5 road from Marble Arch, London, 267 miles distant.

A quarter-mile along Victoria Road, the church of Saint Cybi stands proudly aloft, within the walls of a Roman fort – Caergybi – built originally to provide protection from invasion. Entry is via the north gate in the fourth-century Roman wall, its stones in successive courses canted first one way and then the other to give an unusual 'herringbone' effect. The elevated churchyard provides a fine view of the Old Harbour, with Stena Line's enormous ferries coming and going and much port activity around the ferry berth.

From the bridge spanning the main line into Holyhead station, there is a good view of the station complex which includes the Stena Line office, fronted by a conspicuous clock tower commemorating the opening of the Old Harbour extension by the Prince of Wales in 1880, and of the curved station platform that now marks the end of the line from London. Beyond the station there lies a vast marshalling area for lorries, coaches and cars awaiting their ferries to Ireland. Some passengers and vehicles join the Dún Laoghaire ferry at its berth in the Old Harbour while others are directed onward to Salt Island to join the Dublin ferry. From a roundabout beyond the wide bridge, the route follows Turkey Shore Road, running parallel to the marshalling area north-eastwards to a small dock for fishing vessels at the entrance to the Old Harbour.

Apart from the ferries, various other vessels call at Holyhead: ore carriers, naval ships, fishing boats, coastal tankers, cruise liners large and small, and even the occasional sail-training vessel.

To the south-east, a walk of less than a mile along grassy coastal paths leads to a small but pleasant bay with a sandy beach, known locally as Traeth Penrhos. Nearby, beyond the busy A5, is the extensive works of Anglesey Aluminium Metal Ltd with its gigantic 'landmark' chimney. The plant produces over 100,000 tons of aluminium each year from the

Sail-training vessel at Holyhead

The parish church of Saint Cybi

alumina powder, sucked from ships' holds at its specialised berth in the harbour and conveyed via a tunnel directly to the factory.

For the next two miles the route follows the seaward margin of Penrhos Country Park, a delightful walk. Previously known as Plas Penrhos and, until sold in 1948, home to Lord Stanley of Alderley and his descendants for nearly two hundred years, the estate was resold to Anglesey Aluminium in 1969. The Stanleys were of considerable importance to the development of Holyhead during the eighteenth and nineteenth centuries. In their turn, Anglesey Aluminium have supported the area in the creation of a nature reserve on their land to the east of the A5. Retired policeman Ken Williams, MBE, an amateur naturalist, was the leading light in its development: he set up a sanctuary where injured birds are cared for until they can be released back into the wild.

On the path from the Country Park to join the A5 road heading south-east stands a toll house similar to the one in Llanfair-pwll, unmistakably the work of Thomas Telford. Indeed, he was responsible for the design and construction of the causeway, not quite a mile long, that joins Holy Island to mainland Anglesey. The causeway, which traverses the northern end of the 'Inland Sea', is known as the Stanley Embankment and carries both of the original London-Holyhead lines of communication, the A5 road and the railway, separated from each other by a high stone wall. Ahead, on mainland Anglesey, lie areas of housing at Valley and Newlands Park, while low-lying agricultural land stretches away northward to Carmel Head.

Old A5 toll house

Across the Stanley Embankment

From the Stanley Embankment to Cemlyn Bay

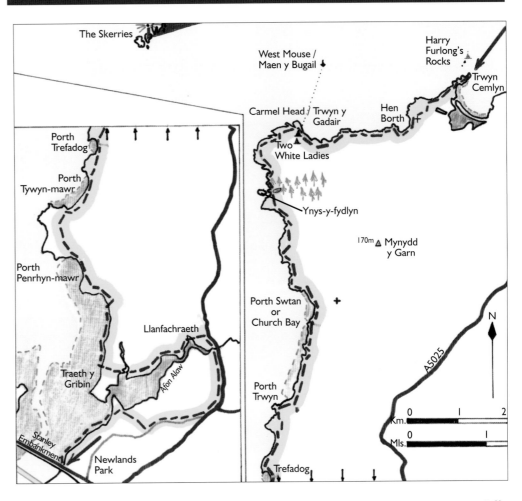

In which we take an early detour to cross Afon Alaw and then encounter cliffs composed of glacial deposits. We see a genuine cruck house at Trefadog, the island's last thatched cottage at Church Bay, the menacing Skerries lurking offshore and a rock-solid coastline as we approach wild and lonely Carmel Head. The contrast to peaceful and enchanting Cemlyn Bay could not be more marked.

Tuffs

Friendly cows

Wild thyme

This section starts along a shingly beach, tide permitting, from the Anglesey end of the Stanley Embankment and right away there is a surprise: the native green mica schist has become purple in places. At low tide, extensive muddy sands and small outcrops of rock are exposed to seaward, along with remnants of a stone-walled fish-trap similar to those in the Menai Strait. At the top of the beach, rows of stone-filled gabions have been placed against the low cliffs of glacial deposits, to resist erosion by the sea, a matter of concern to nearby home-owners. Soon, the houses give way to open farmland, but then, half a mile or so further on, the shallow and rather muddy estuary of Afon Alaw poses a challenge. It could be dangerous to wade across, even at low tide, and, as there is no recognised footpath along the Alaw's

southern bank, the only safe thing to do is to take one of the paths leading south-eastwards up to the country road between Newlands Park and Llanynghenedl.

Onward next along the A5025, crossing Afon Alaw at Llanfachraeth and a turning left at the village post-office-cum-store leads back to the sea on the north side of the Alaw estuary by way of a small bridge and reasonably good footpaths. Grazing cattle and sheep occupy the fields on both sides of the estuary but, apart from a few ducks, waders and the call of a lone curlew, the landscape is empty. Afon Alaw might look more inviting at high tide but it is doubtful that it will ever justify a four-mile diversion in order to progress a mere half mile! Throughout this stage of the walk Anglesey Aluminium's chimney and Holyhead Mountain are rarely out of sight and the busy ferries are clearly visible rounding the end of the Holyhead breakwater.

Traeth y Gribin is a large beach littered with common seashells, washed in from Holyhead Bay, including razor, cockle, gaper, limpet and mussel. A promontory separates Traeth y Gribin from the next bay, Porth Penrhyn-mawr, and it is probably better to follow the signposted track leading through fields and over the top of the headland. Dropping down into the much smaller Porth Penrhyn-mawr, the extensive layout of Penrhyn Caravan Park looms up ahead: beyond lies an alien environment of concrete roadways, mown verges and neat stone walls, followed by a large, highly-mechanised, tidy and prosperous-looking farm. Then, after a further half mile along a precise metalled lane, comes the caravan park itself with row upon row of well-maintained and neatly parked caravans near the large and very fine beach of Porth Tywyn-mawr.

Another headland next (actually a glacial drumlin), with wild flowers and good views in all directions, and then another bay; this time it's Porth Trefadog and, on the way are the visible remains of an early medieval coastal promontory fort though possibly the motte dates back to Iron Age times. There's a change in the shoreline rocks here, from the green mica schist to beige-coloured tuffs of volcanic origin which continue for the next three miles or so. These rocks were formed from ash that rained down following an explosive volcanic eruption. No more than half a dozen properties remain at Trefadog now, along with a few discreet caravans, but the place is geometrically neat, has character – it once provided simple port facilities for a nearby medieval settlement. Centrally, above the beach, there is a modern farm attached to a striking thirteenth-century residence named 'Trefadog'. This is a genuine cruck house and is one of the oldest properties in Anglesey. At the northern end of the bay, a flight of wooden steps climbs to a newly-fenced, good-walking path around the perimeter of the next headland, which drops down to a stony and rock-strewn bay of no apparent name. At a car park above this beach, the path becomes a single-track road heading uphill away from the bay, thereby avoiding a headland property which boasts a collection of elderly road vehicles and other machinery. There is even a wrecked fishing vessel lying on Carreg-y-frân and it is not clear whether this is part of the collection or a genuine maritime misadventure.

Swtan cottage

Quarter of a mile up the hill, a 'tern' coastal-path sign takes the walker back towards the sea to join a cliff-top footpath leading into the Porth Trwyn area. The direct route from this point bypasses the bay altogether, proceeds behind several bungalows and more or less in a straight line northward. But Porth Trwyn is a very pleasant sandy bay, and, if the tide is low, there is an alternative route across the beach which climbs back up to the coastal path from its northern end. From here on, the route is very easy to follow. There are several inlets on the way up to Porth Swtan (Church Bay) providing regular glimpses of cobbled beaches and rocks below while, at path level, occasional dwellings stand within the adjacent farmland. Porth Crugmor is interesting, where the path drops down to sea level in order to cross a freshwater stream, alongside a very neat and appealing bungalow.

Vikings, Invaders and Settlers

The Old Norse word *sker* means a small rocky reef or island, and this is where the Skerries, sparsely-vegetated islands lying two miles offshore from Carmel Head, originally derive their name, though their Welsh title *Ynysoedd y Moelrhoniaid* (Islands of the Bald-headed Grey Seals) gives a more instantly-recognisable description. There are many other echoes of Anglesey's Viking legacy in its place-names, 'Anglesey' itself coming originally from '*Ongulsey*' or Ongull's Island.

Initially the object of opportunistic plundering forays, Anglesey became a more serious prize once the Danes had settled bases in the Isle of Man and Ireland. During the ninth century, there began a long series of raids on Anglesey which were a constant concern to the Princes of Gwynedd, especially Rhodri Mawr, or Rhodri the Great. After a devastating attack by the Danes in 854, Rhodri struck back in 856, winning an important victory and killing the Danish leader, Gorm. Sadly, however, it wasn't long before Rhodri was forced to flee to Ireland, in 877, after fighting another battle on Anglesey, this time unsuccessful, against the Norse invaders.

He and his son, Gwriad, were said to have been killed shortly afterwards by Saxons under the leadership of Alfred the Great, ironically one of only two other leaders in that century to earn the epithet 'Great'.

Ynys Seiriol or Priestholm

timewatch

Early Times

Neolithic burial sites, and the remains of hut circles such as Din Lligwy and hillforts such as Caer y Twr are evidence of early occupation.

circa 100-400

Despite the Roman failure to colonise the island after Suetonius' invasion in AD 61, the walls of a Roman fort at Caergybi can still be seen, enclosing today's parish church.

from circa 400

In a rather more peaceful 'invasion', Christian missionary saints from about the fifth century onwards established religious foundations on the island.

600-1282

Norse raiders threatened the firm rule of the Gwynedd princes; yet it was Viking resistance which halted the advance of William the Conqueror's Norman forces at the Menai Strait.

1295

After the death of Llywelyn ap Gruffudd, Edward I of England began work on the mighty castle at Beaumaris as part of his campaign to protect his newly-won territories.

STRANGE REVERSALS

Who would have thought that the Vikings, responsible so long for raiding and plundering Anglesey's riches, would ultimately come to the island's rescue? However, in 1098 a Viking fleet led by the quaintly-named Magnus Barelegs halted the advance of William the Conqueror's Norman forces at the Menai Strait.

SEIRIOL WYN·SEIRIOL WHITE

CYBI FELYN CYBI TAWNY

Perhaps fate took an even stranger hand when Ynys Seiriol became known for a while by its Scandinavian name, Priestholm, once the Norsemen, after years of targeting Anglesey's monasteries and churches, eventually converted to Christianity.

Then, back at cliff level again, a short walk leads to the picturesque village at Porth Swtan, or Church Bay. The Welsh name relates to the species of fish – the *swtan* or 'whiting-pout' – once commonly caught in these waters, whereas the English name derives simply from the conspicuous spired church of Saint Rhuddlad which overlooks the village.

Nearly all the village buildings are painted white; of special interest is Cyfeillion Swtan which is the last thatched cottage remaining in Anglesey. In 1999, it was restored as part of a training scheme in traditional building skills and then opened to the public as a folk museum. And just across the road is a well-known sea-food restaurant called The Lobster Pot. (Lobster pots abound off this rocky coastline. Clearly, not all the catch goes for export.) The village road ends abruptly at the coastline with a steep ramp leading down to a large and attractive beach of sand and shingle. Here, rotted pyroclastic rocks, or tuffs, of a striking honey colour form the cliffs behind the northern part of the beach.

The next section involves a subtle change: the cliffs become higher and the path is slightly further from the sea. Not quite moorland because the land is mostly farmed, but there is a feeling of 'wide open space' on this stretch up to Trwyn y Gadair, (Carmel Head). The path leaving Church Bay is well-defined and provides an excellent view down to the bay. The headlands and several of the fields to the east of the path are close-cropped by sheep, but there are also fields of oats and grass grown for winter feed. Wild flowers and insects are plentiful. After the long sweep of Porth-y-bribys and the trek across Trwyn y Crewyn, it comes as a surprise when the path descends steeply into an east-west valley, with coniferous forest on its north flank and a reed-filled shallow lake along the valley bottom, running down to a small pebbly beach and the 'high water island' of Ynys-y-fydlyn. There's a story that a beautiful young woman called Rhona, daughter of a local Welsh chief, was fleeing from a party of Viking raiders with her young Welsh lover. They managed to scramble across the slippery rocks onto Ynys-y-fydlyn, where the young man had hidden his coracle, but the Vikings were still in hot pursuit. Suddenly, the earth shook with a thunderous sound and the island split across leaving a wide chasm between the young couple and their pursuers. The chasm is there to this day, so it must be true!

Common poppy

Ynys-y-fydlyn

The geology of Carmel Head is renowned not so much for its rock types, but for the fact that the strata are upside down. Ancient Precambrian rocks have been thrust up and over the top of younger Ordovician rocks as a result of some massive upheaval millions of years ago. But the most interesting visual feature actually lies about two miles offshore in the shape of the Skerries. This low-lying and infamous group of rocks is only half a mile in length but, being constantly swept by strong tidal currents, they have become a graveyard for many ships and their crews, including the very first Royal Yacht in 1675. Today's lighthouse, with its fog signal and powerful twenty-mile white light warns vessels to steer well clear.

Carmel Head provides a very solid north-west corner for the Isle of Anglesey, with Porth-y-dyfn marking the only gap in the wall of rock that faces the sea. It is a lonely place and, in a storm, bleak in the extreme. But there's drama in this sweeping landscape, completely empty except for sheep, bracken, some crumbling evidence of a long-forgotten mining attempt and two tall triangular stone-built navigational transit marks, known as 'The Two White Ladies'. They are positioned so as to be precisely in line on the bearing of Maen y Bugail (West Mouse) and Coal Rock.

The path turns a corner at Carmel Head to face eastwards with a new landmark up ahead, the massive rectangular form of Wylfa nuclear power station. Eastward along Anglesey's northern coastline, an easy cliff-top path skirts regular farmland, passing a number of small stony beaches, separated by small headlands. Hen Borth is the only sizable bay. Reefs of rock run out seaward all along this coast to Trwyn Cemlyn. The receding tide uncovers several offshore ledges upon which seals haul out and 'sing' while groups of cormorant air their wings and discuss the day's catch. Ashore, a frenzy of butterflies is attracted to the knapweed and an isolated little church turns up in the middle of acres of farmland. This is the church of Llanrhwydrys and it is thought that a place of worship has stood upon the same site since the twelfth century.

Finally, the coastal path descends to Trwyn Cemlyn, at the entrance to Cemlyn Bay. Offshore lies a group of treacherous rocks known as Cerrig Brith or Harry Furlong's Rocks. Did Harry find and mark the reef or did he perish there? Either way, Trwyn Cemlyn concludes the long walk from the Stanley Embankment.

Hen Borth, towards Cemlyn

Llanrhwydrys church

VIII From Cemlyn Bay to Porth Wen

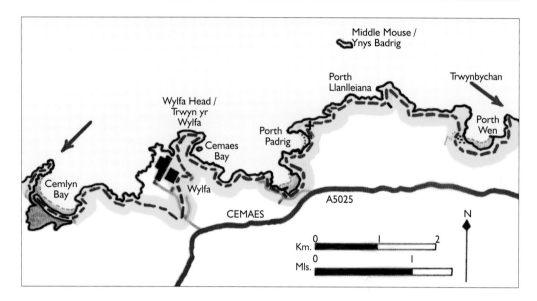

In which we enjoy the charm and beauty of Cemlyn Bay, Cemaes Bay, Porth Wen and a unique church, all merging comfortably with remnants of bygone industries and in stark contrast to a modern nuclear power station and a growing 'forest' of wind turbines.

The harnessing of wind power reminds us of Anglesey's exposure to the elements and the dreadful loss of life from shipwrecks along its dangerous coastline, almost inevitable until Frances Williams devoted the proceeds of her artistic talent to set up, with her husband, a local lifeboat service. Seafarers in general and citizens of Anglesey can be thankful for Frances Williams and proud of the fact that her talent echoed through a further three generations to one of the island's most famous sons, the late Sir Kyffin Williams RA.

A Wylfa pylon

Field scabious at Porth Wen

Pebbles at Cemlyn

Cemlyn Bay is such a neat coastal feature, peaceful and enchanting, provided that the dominance of Wylfa nuclear power station can be overlooked. Starting from Trwyn Cemlyn, the path follows the western shore of the bay. Green mica schist, cut by numerous dykes, and golden sand form an attractive geological combination and provide an interesting beach for young and old alike. A simple stone plaque commemorates the first lifeboat to be launched in Wales, in 1828, at this very spot. Local subscription paid for the much-needed boat, propelled by oars – there was probably no better protected north-coast launching site than this cove in Cemlyn Bay.

Across the head of the bay stretches a massive curved shingle spit, set up by storm waves and separating the bay itself from the brackish nature-reserve lagoon, reached by crossing a small weir, adjacent to some strangely walled-in buildings. It seems that the original owner was a pioneer aviator, a racing car driver and a keen ornithologist. For many years he managed the lagoon and nature reserve as part of his private estate and it is said that he built the high walls around his home as shelter for his garden birds. The lagoon is visited by a great variety of sea birds with some, like the visiting terns, nesting on a small island in the lagoon during the summer months and feeding their chicks upon sand eels which the parent birds catch with ease in the confused seas out at Harry Furlong's Rocks. Winter time sees wigeon, tufted duck and golden-eye taking over the lagoon, while at various times of the year, black-headed gulls, lapwing, stonechat, skylark and even a family of swans may put in an appearance. Walking the spit on its seaward side is quite heavy going as the deep shingle is rather unstable. The combination of storm waves and different tide levels has created terraces in the shingle but its real enchantment lies at the water's edge where rounded and polished pebbles, tumbled by the waves, wet and glistening in the sunlight, exhibit every possible hue.

From this enchanting bay, the coastal path leads off from the eastern car park, north-eastwards to round a flattish headland and enter Porth-y-pistyll. Here the terrain is low-lying, mostly covered by gorse, heather and fern. There are small shingly beaches but it comes as a surprise to stumble upon 'Anglesey's best kept secret': Cestyll ornamental gardens, tucked away with an old water-mill beside a stream that flows through the grounds. These are now Wylfa power station's responsibility, but they used to be part of Lady Astor's estate and are open to the public once or twice a year. Opened back in 1972, the nuclear-fuelled power station's technology is by no means new, yet it still generates enough electricity to meet the demands of two large cities and is expected to continue operating at full capacity until 2010. The electrical energy is conveyed down a line of huge pylons that stride off across Anglesey, crossing the Menai Strait alongside the Britannia Bridge.

After digesting much technical information at the Visitor Centre, along with a *panad* of tea or coffee, it is time to move on. The route now links up with a pleasant nature trail through Wylfa's wooded grounds, climbing up to an observation point with a good view of the extent of the power station. The underlying rocks are all Precambrian green schists that were formed about 600 million years ago, so they are not likely to go anywhere, which is just as well because each of Wylfa's two reactors weighs 84,000 tons!

Just below and beyond this observation point, at the car park, the coastal path offers a choice: either northwards to Trwyn yr Wylfa (Wylfa Head) or eastwards to Cemaes. Given good weather and visibility, the diversion to Wylfa Head with its striking panoramic views is worth the extra mile. The headland itself is rather exposed and barren but, on its eastern flank, there is a splendid view of the full extent of Cemaes Bay and a pleasant beach at Porth yr Ogof – a good place to stop for sandwiches.

Swans on the lagoon

Rejoining the route to Cemaes, the path sets out across some large fields full of thistles that attract a variety of bees and other insects. Then, on reaching Porth Wylfa (yet another rock and shingle bay, but very well defined), the path switches to a cliff-top route leading down into the centre of the delightful one-time fishing village of Cemaes. Because sea transport was the only real option at the time, its little harbour was developed at various stages during the nineteenth century to keep pace with local economic growth. Sailing vessels berthed to discharge cargoes of coal and sailed again, carrying limestone, corn, marble, bricks, lime and ochre. Local activity was also influenced by developments in the booming copper town of Amlwch, barely five miles to the east, and so, to help meet demand, ships of up to 400 tons were built at Cemaes before road and rail developments overtook transportation by sea.

The artist Sir Kyffin Williams writing about his great-grandparents James and Frances Williams.

'As a bride, Frances began her long association with the sea when she came to her husband's rectory at Llanfair-yng-Nghornwy, where the waves race and roar, and jagged reefs, such as the Harry Furlongs, wait to rip open the bottoms of the ships that pass between the Skerries and the mainland. There were continual disasters, the first of which occurred as soon as the couple arrived back from their honeymoon. A packet boat, the *Alert*, struck the West Mouse rock and, buffeted by the racing tide, gradually broke up . . .

Whether the thought came to them simultaneously I do not know, but from that moment onwards they were determined that there should always be boats ready to prevent such disasters. James exhorted the local gentry; Frances started a fund to buy lifeboats and reward those who saved lives, and made lithographs to raise money.'

Kyffin Williams, *Across the Straits*

SIR KYFFIN WILLIAMS

✠ Born in Llangefni in 1918

✠ Educated at Shrewsbury School and at the Slade School of Art

✠ Served with the Royal Welsh Fusiliers from 1936 to 1941

✠ Taught at Highgate School, London

✠ In 1968 won a Winston Churchill Scholarship to Patagonia

✠ Elected a member of the Royal Academy in 1974

✠ Retrospective exhibition in 1987 at the National Museum of Wales, Cardiff

✠ Received numerous civil and academic honours

✠ Knighted in 1999

✠ Died in 2006

CODWYD Y GOFEB HON
I DDATHLU
CAN MLWYDD A HANNER
SEFYDLU A LANSIO'R
BAD–ACHUB CYNTAF AR
YNYS MÔN
1828 – 1978
SEFYDLWYD GAN Y PARCH. JAMES WILLIAMS
A FRANCES WILLIAMS
ERECTED TO COMMEMORATE
THE ONE HUNDRED AND FIFTIETH
ANNIVERSARY OF ESTABLISHING
AND LAUNCHING THE FIRST
LIFE BOAT
ON THE ISLE OF ANGLESEY
1828 – 1978
ESTABLISHED BY THE REV. JAMES WILLIAMS
AND FRANCES WILLIAMS
(RENOVATED BY WYLFA
POWER STATION. JUNE 1998)

The industrial heyday for Cemaes passed and today's charming village and harbour has probably changed little in the last hundred years except in its growing attraction for holiday-makers. Little if any fishing industry remains, except for lobster catchers, and the tidy little half-tide harbour is now occupied mainly by pleasure craft. Cemaes is such a well-kept and happy place, with an interesting main street and a pleasant sandy beach.

At headland level above the eastern end of the beach, there are still westward glimpses of Wylfa's nuclear power station. To the south, however, twenty-four turbines of the Rhyd-y-gors windfarm, each thirty metres high, stand in the view behind Cemaes, supplying about 6,000 homes with electricity, provided the wind blows. Northwards, cattle graze the headlands but the farmland is interrupted by quarried gorges where limestone and marble were extracted in the eighteenth century. There is a good path across the headlands but it is worth dropping down onto the beach at Porth Padrig, to see the colourful mixture of rocks described as a 'mélange' by geologist Edward Greenly author of *The Geology of Anglesey* (Vol. I & II), published in 1919. Back up on the northerly headland, the route leads east to Llanbadrig church amid a congregation of wild flowers.

Saint Patrick is well-remembered in these parts. Apparently, having suffered shipwreck on Ynys Badrig (Middle Mouse) while on passage to Ireland, Bishop Patrick struggled ashore and, thankful to have survived, he had a small wooden cliff-top church built overlooking the scene of his misadventure. There have been various rebuilds of Llanbadrig church over the years and the top of the present font dates back to the twelfth century. By 1840, extensive and expensive church restoration was required and it was the third Lord Stanley of Alderley, a well-known figure in Anglesey, who put up the money on condition that the new interior should reflect his own Muslim faith. Thus this charming little Christian parish church presents some unique features reminiscent of a mosque: striking blue, red and white stained glass, a blue-tiled sanctuary and Pastor Bonus mosaic. Its setting, high on the headland, with the graveyard overlooking the Irish Sea, is breathtaking.

Steep climbs and descents lie ahead as the cliffs and headlands become bigger and bolder on the way to Porth Wen. Tall, dense bracken covers a lot of the route, obscuring much of the ground detail, even the path at times, but somehow delicate harebells find room to reach for the sun. Offshore, the Middle Mouse

Cemaes harbour

Llanbadrig church

in outline justifies its English name, while the ebb tide races past to the west. How did Saint Patrick ever manage to get across?

The run of spectacular cliffs culminates in the biggest of them all at the entrance to Porth Llanlleiana, getting on for 200 feet up to Dinas Gynfor, once the site of an Iron Age hill-fort. In the ravine leading to Llanlleiana beach there's an unexpected sight, the ruin of a once elegant limestone-built china clay works. Hydrated aluminium silicate was dug out nearby, refined at the works and then exported by sea. At the top of a steep zigzag path passing the works' chimney, the route turns northwards along the promontory to a derelict watchtower-cum-summer-house, given the name 'Coronation Tower' to commemorate the accession of Edward VII. This is the northernmost point of Anglesey (and Wales), and on a really clear day, the mountains of Mourne in Ireland, the Isle of Man and Cumbria may be seen from here. From Coronation Tower, a gentle descent steepens considerably towards Porth Cynfor or Hell's Mouth, well-named from the point of view of someone trying to beach a sailing vessel in anything other than a flat calm! But the last half mile to Torllwyn, a headland guarding the entrance to Porth Wen, is fairly straightforward and the views across and into the bay are delightful.

Porth Wen is a three-sided bay formed by a deep bite into the northern cliffs. Relatively inaccessible and secluded, it is a peaceful and rather special place. The shoreline of rock gives way to a pinkish shingle beach at the head of the bay. Farms and green fields extend right to the cliff edge in places but what catches the eye more than anything else is the derelict brickworks tucked into the western shore of the bay. The coastal path bypasses the works but, with care, it is possible to scramble down through the gorse to look at this interesting site where quartzite from the nearby cliffs was used to make silica bricks for the steel industry's furnaces until the operation closed in 1914. The deserted brickworks, its angular quay, beehive ovens and tall chimneys all have their own appeal, particularly in the evening sunlight. The onward path skirts the perimeter of the bay, crossing a number of fields, passing behind Castell farm and then climbing north-eastwards to Trwynbychan, bringing the eighth stage to a close on Porth Wen's eastern headland.

China clay works

Porth Wen brickworks

IX From Porth Wen to Lligwy Bay

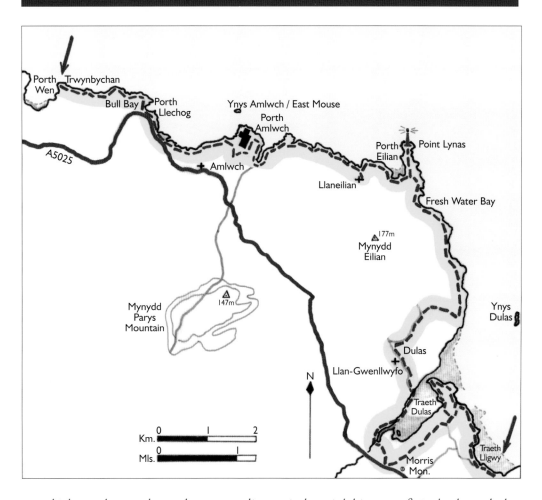

In which we learn about the extraordinary industrial history of Amlwch and the mysteries of an 'occulting' lighthouse. We visit two churches with remarkable interiors and contents and also hear about a family of famous brothers, Morrisiaid Môn. We discover the origins of Devonian Old Red Sandstone and learn about the archaeological remains at Din Lligwy.

Bryony

Bull Bay

Cave in Porth Llechog

An easy and enjoyable walk next through clumps of heather and gorse though slightly less dramatic cliff scenery. The rocks in these parts are tuffs (consolidated volcanic ash). Soon the path begins to descend to a lower level as it approaches Porth Llechog. This part of Anglesey's coastline is well-known among birdwatchers for sightings of fulmars or, further out, graceful gannets circling and gliding above the waves. The village of Bull Bay, tucked into the sheltered western corner of Porth Llechog, took its name from a nearby deep pool, Pwll-y-tarw or the Bull Pool. Once engaged in fishing and shipbuilding, Bull Bay's main livelihood today is tourism; quietly picturesque, it boasts the most northerly golf course in Wales, built in 1913 by the sixth Marquess of Anglesey.

Bull Bay's size is deceptive: it is larger than is evident at first sight from its little cove at sea level. A straightforward walk above the cliffs lies ahead; the view includes Ynys Amlwch or East Mouse (completing the set of three 'rodent' islets off the north coast), together with a somewhat 'industrial' first impression of Amlwch. Its meteoric rise to prosperity during the last thirty years of the eighteenth century, from a hamlet of six fishermen's cottages to a boom-town with a population of around 6,000, resulted from two natural phenomena: firstly, the discovery in 1768 of rich veins of high-grade copper ore in the felsite rock at Parys Mountain, just two miles south of the hamlet; and secondly, Amlwch's small natural harbour, formed by a narrow but deep cleft in the local green mica schist, facilitating transport of the mined copper ore by sea.

Amlwch was fortunate in having a new and rapidly expanding market for its copper. Wooden ships, particularly naval vessels, were adopting the practice of sheathing their hulls with thin copper plate below the waterline to combat the attentions of the teredo worm (*Tinavalis*), and of marine growth generally. This considerably increased demand for copper! While copper mining was undoubtedly the town's mainstay, a broad range of ancillary industries together with numerous businesses linked to the mining and smelting of copper provided Amlwch with enviable employment opportunities, though with a number of attendant social problems, such as poverty and drunkenness. A brewery had to be established in the town just to keep up with demand from the numerous taverns!

Imagine, for a moment, a long line of horse-drawn carts, laden with ore, trundling down from Parys Mountain through the town and down again to this remarkable little harbour in its rocky gorge. In the early days the harbour would have been busy with small commercial sailing vessels loading ore from dockside bins, while others were still discharging their limestone ballast to be burned in the kilns to produce agricultural lime. Later on, however, it was realised that smelting the copper ore on-site was also good business. But this expansion involved a huge amount of additional traffic: there would have been vessels waiting at anchor, vessels berthing, vessels sailing; congestion in the dock, congestion on the quayside; the little port simply could not cope with such burgeoning activity and so its capacity had to be increased by an Act of Parliament in 1793. With the additional establishment of two shipbuilding enterprises by the turn of the century, Amlwch was humming.

After the collapse of the copper trade by the mid-nineteenth century, Amlwch had to wait until the 1970s for a new major industrial project, in the shape of an offshore deep-water terminal where very large oil tankers could discharge their cargoes of oil through a system of seabed pipelines to the shore and thence, via nearly eighty miles of buried pipeline, to the Stanlow refinery in Cheshire. The oil industry's presence brought several improvements, including a new breakwater, more berths in the harbour and an excellent heritage museum housed in the old sail loft, but the operation itself was short-lived and shut down in 1987. The last conspicuous industry to come

Amlwch's way was the chemical plant, west of the harbour. The product was bromine, extracted from sea water, but yet again there were problems and production ceased in 2004.

Along the coastal path, from Amlwch to Porth Eilian, it is pleasant walking over grassy paths and around rocky outcrops. To the east lies the conspicuous promontory of Point Lynas with its white-painted lighthouse and associated buildings. To seaward there may be a glimpse of the dolphins that now patrol these waters. Depending upon the time of high tide at Liverpool's docks, large ships may be seen close in at Point Lynas with a high-speed pilot boat scurrying between them. Inward-bound vessels can pick up their Liverpool pilots here while outward-bounders drop their pilots off.

Welcome to Amlwch

Amlwch harbour

Fraught-iron anchor!

In the vicinity of Porthyrychen, a pyramidal spire heralds Saint Eilian's church. Saint Eilian and his family travelled by ship from Rome in the sixth century and came ashore at Porthyrychen. He built his oratory on the site and became famous for his remarkable powers in curing a variety of human disorders. In the twelfth century a church was built on the site of his shrine and dedicated to him. Only the tower and unusual spire remain but today's church is most interesting with its carved rood screens and Saint Eilian's chapel. Further along the coastal path, by the beach at Porth Eilian, a storyboard gives a detailed account of the saint's exploits.

The 'lighthouse' road takes the walker up to a promontory offering lovely views of the coast as well as the countryside sweeping down from Mynydd Eilian. From Point Lynas, with its eighteen-mile 'occulting' lighthouse (the fixed white light is shut off at regular intervals), the trend of the coastline abruptly changes direction again from east to south-south-east, running down to Traeth Coch (Red Wharf Bay). Pilot boats on the Lynas station are normally based at Amlwch but, on the east side of the promontory, a modern steel structure can be seen at the water's edge, providing a sheltered landing stage for a pilot boat when westerly weather conditions might otherwise cause suspension of the service. Ahead lies a three-mile walk down past Fresh Water Bay and on to Traeth Dulas. This is a somewhat lonely stretch of coastline with steeply-undulating sheep fields sweeping down to the cliff tops from inland hills that rise to 500 feet and more. The climb up above Fresh Water Bay offers a magnificent view down to Point Lynas although the way through tall bracken is not always obvious and occasional notices warn of footpath closures in the autumn and winter for pheasant shoots.

At Ynys Dulas, a reef of rock with a stone-built beacon, the route turns inland along a line of Scots pine trees, avoiding the Llysdulas estate but affording occasional glimpses of stately dwellings. A tree-lined country road skirts the estate and leads downhill to a scattering of houses at Dulas and the shore at Dulas Bay. Nearby stands the church of Saint Gwenllwyfo with its tall, slender steeple and an exceptionally neat and tidy churchyard. With clean lines and full of light, the church's most memorable feature is its sixteenth-century stained-glass windows and panels from a Carthusian monastery in Louvain, purchased for the church by the owners of the Llysdulas estate.

St Eilian's church spire and rood screen

Point Lynas lighthouse

Dried-out precipitation ponds

Parys Mountain

Viewed from a distance, there is nothing remarkable about this 500-foot hill, a mere two miles south of Amlwch. But at close quarters amid its desolate acidic landscape, where even heather and gorse struggle to survive, it leaves a never-to-be-forgotten impression. For just thirty years at the end of the eighteenth century, coinciding with the early years of the Industrial Revolution, some 1,500 Anglesey miners worked the mountain's body of copper ore; they led the world in the production of copper and brought great but transient prosperity to Amlwch.

Different methods of extraction were employed. Initially, shafts were sunk, with underground tunnels chasing the veins of copper, but then the miners turned to opencast operations resulting in huge cavernous workings in the central region of the mountain, all the more dramatic for the startling range of colours from mineral oxidation among the rocks and spoil heaps.

The peak yield of about 80,000 tons of ore annually was increased by the method of extraction known as precipitation. It had long been known that natural streams running down from Parys Mountain carried copper salts in solution. The older workings were therefore flooded with water which, as it drained through the rocks, became a solution of copper sulphate and this was collected at lower levels in a number of brick-lined ponds. Scrap iron thrown into these ponds, together with a neat bit of chemistry, resulted in the precipitation of fine crystals of copper.

Amlwch also benefited from a number of by-products from the mining operation, including lead, silver, zinc and sulphur, while the ponds yielded a residue of yellow ochre for the manufacture of paint. All too soon, however, decline set in as Parys Mountain ran out of quality ore; also, at the end of the Napoleonic wars, demand fell and cheaper African and American copper became available. Fifteen years into the new century and Amlwch's amazing copper trade had almost collapsed, unemployment followed and the town suffered. A few mines took advantage of sporadic recoveries in the market but, by 1850, it was virtually all over.

Locked entrance to old workings

from 2000 BC

Parys Mountain has been a copper-mining site since prehistoric times. Evidence of firesetting to fracture rock faces has been found and also tools fashioned from stone and antler.

from AD 100

The Romans mined copper at Parys Mountain, probably using slave labour, but all mined ore automatically belonged to the Roman State.

1564

In an attempt to revive Britain's copper industry, Elizabeth I established the 'Company of the Mines Royal', with exclusive rights to copper mining in Wales.

1768

After many years of indifferent prospecting at Parys Mountain, Derbyshire miner Jonathan Roose took on the search and, on 2 March, located the huge body of ore that would make Amlwch famous.

1775

Local lawyer Thomas Williams kept the peace between the two owners of Parys Mountain, Sir Nicholas Bayly and the Rev Edward Hughes, bringing benefit to Amlwch and earning him two unofficial titles: the 'Copper King' and 'Twm Chwarae Teg' (Tom Fair Play)!

AMLWCH
Tref Gopr Hynafol
The Ancient Copper Town

THE COPPER LADIES

As the miners toiled in the precarious depths below, lumps of ore-bearing rock were loaded into buckets, hoisted to the surface and then barrowed to nearby sheds on the hillside. Within these long sheds, as many as eighty women, known locally as Copper Ladies, sat in rows facing each other and had the task of breaking down the rock to retrieve the valuable ore, discarding the remainder to spoil heaps.

Conditions for the Copper Ladies would not have been pleasant; they trudged daily up to the hillside sheds in all weathers for a twelve-hour shift amid choking dust and noise. By all accounts, however, they were ever cheerful and were renowned for their incessant chatter! A kind of uniform evolved, for in addition to their basic warm clothing, each woman wore a black hat, a spotted yellow scarf to keep out the dust and grit, a leather apron and gloves with each finger protected by iron rings. Her equipment amounted only to a square block of iron upon which she broke down the rock, a four-pound brick-hammer and a basket into which she dropped hand-sized pieces of quality ore.

From the sheds the ore was taken to be roasted in kilns, to remove its sulphur content. Roasting the ore could take weeks but, as the presence of sulphur hindered smelting, it was essential. (It also enabled retrieval of sulphur as a marketable by-product.) Now cinder-like in appearance, the roasted ore was then crushed and ground before the final smelting process to release metallic copper.

Broadsheet ballad praising the virtues of the Copper Ladies

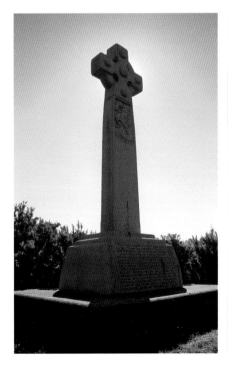

The Morris cross

Pilot Boat Inn

Traeth Lligwy

Traeth Dulas is an almost land-locked bay of sand and mud, measuring roughly one mile in length and half a mile across. Apart from a couple of streams flowing through it, the bay spends most of its life dry and remote from the sea. Only at high tide does any significant sea water enter and only at spring tides does it fill right up. Historically, however, the protection that Dulas Bay afforded to small commercial sailing vessels against severe weather from any quarter made it quite important. Clay was excavated from the north shore and sailing colliers brought in coal for the brickworks. Limestone was shipped in for burning in the kilns and, when bad weather prevented loading at Amlwch, copper ore was carted to Dulas Bay for shipment. Some shipbuilding also took place here but, today, it is

doubtful if anything more venturesome than bird-watching occurs within the bay. Shipwreck was such a common event on Anglesey's shores, before the days of steam, that the beacon on Ynys Dulas reef in the approaches to Dulas Bay was built to double as a shelter for mariners who might be stranded there, complete with a supply of food and drink. The coastal path route follows the shoreline of the bay, heading south-westwards; it then crosses a marsh and a field before joining a lane that leads to the main road, the A5025. Then, after only a few yards on the road, behind the Pilot Boat Inn, a stile leads to fields and higher ground to the south of Traeth Dulas.

A couple of hundred yards on the left, beyond the stile at the Pilot Boat Inn, is a cluster of farm buildings called Pentre-eiriannell. This was home to the eighteenth-century Morris family whose four sons, Lewis, Richard, William and John became known locally as *Morrisiaid Môn*. Their impact upon Welsh literature and history was enormous. Young John sadly was lost at sea but the other three kept in close touch through their letters to each other. Collectively, their hundreds of letters provide a rich commentary upon life in Anglesey at that time. Lewis was both practical and scholarly. Had he prepared his *curriculum vitae*, it would have included: hydrographic surveyor, engineer, mineralogist, poet, historian, local government official and publisher (he even attempted to set up a printing press). On behalf of the Admiralty, he produced the first accurate navigational charts of the coast of Wales with no more equipment than a boat, magnetic compass and lead-line. His chart of the west coast of Wales is particularly interesting because it is drawn 'west up', so that Cardigan Bay stretches horizontally across the chart. It was also drawn before chronometers were readily available to mariners, who therefore had no shipboard means of determining their longitude. In consequence, the chart carries a scale of latitude, but no longitude. Brothers Richard and William were rather in Lewis's shadow, but still most accomplished and influential. A monument to the remarkable brothers, in the form of a Celtic cross, stands up on the hill to the right, amid the gorse.

A north-eastward, mile-long trek over the hill leads back to the coastline. The distinctive outline of Ynys Dulas comes into view again and then, if the tide is out, the golden sands of Traeth yr Ora. South-eastwards a pleasant walk along beaches or low cliff tops leads to Lligwy Bay. There are some truly lovely beaches along the way but then comes Traeth Lligwy itself, bigger than all of them put together, with car parks and room for everyone. At the approach to the bay, there are several extensive exposures of Old Red Sandstone dating back to the Devonian period and with quite a story to tell. Around 370 million years ago, pebbles, sand, silt and mud accumulated under sub-tropical conditions in what was probably a large mountain-flanked valley, subject to seasonal rainfall and occasional floods, that lay in the southern hemisphere. The bulk of the deposits were laid down by rivers but some accumulated in semi-permanent lakes whilst others represent former screes. Some of the siltstones also contain calcareous (limestone)

Beached schooner, Dulas Bay

nodules, typical of soils forming under a warm climate and experiencing seasonal rainfall. Following the formation of the layers of conglomerate, sandstone, siltstone and mudstone and during the slow – less than an inch a year – but steady northward drift of one of the Earth's ancient tectonic plates of which they formed a part, the largely red, iron-stained rocks were folded during a period of powerful earth movements. These tectonic forces lifted and tilted the beds of rock so that they now dip at quite a steep angle to the south-east. At the other end of Lligwy Bay it is startling to find cliffs of limestone in horizontal beds standing behind a jumble of huge rectangular blocks of the same rock. What an amazing contrast! But the limestone deserves a story all to itself!

At Lligwy there are very well-preserved ancient constructions that overlook the bay, less than a mile distant and easily accessible. The circular and

Old Red Sandstone at Lligwy Bay

Din Lligwy

rectangular limestone wall-foundations of huts at Din Lligwy, within a strong outer enclosure, polygonal in plan, provide an excellent example of a defended settlement that was occupied from pre- to post-Roman times, probably by a chieftain or other important person. Nearby and very much younger are the remains of Capel Lligwy, built originally in the twelfth century. Again of limestone, together with a multiplicity of wave-worn boulders, a mysterious flight of steps leads down to a small crypt. Nearby again, but very much older this time, is a communal burial chamber probably dating back to 2,500 BC. Today the visitor sees a huge limestone slab supported by a circular 'wall' of boulders although, originally, the whole structure was covered by a mound of earth and stones. In each of the Lligwy relics, only the grey-white limestone remains, a reminder that the time scales for rock, both in its formation and its durability, far exceed those of all other natural materials on the planet.

X From Lligwy Bay to Bwrdd Arthur

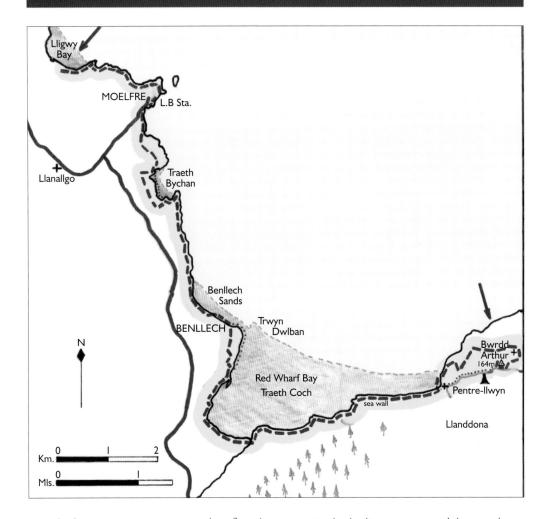

In which we continue our study of geology, particularly limestone, and learn about the 'Royal Charter' wreck, the 'Hindlea' and the courage of Moelfre's famous lifeboat coxswain. Beyond Benllech, we survey the sweep of Red Wharf Bay, hear about the Witches of Llanddona and climb Bwrdd Arthur to enjoy the magnificent views.

Lifeboat coxswain Dic Evans MBE, remembered in bronze at Moelfre

Cottages at Moelfre

Vetch

Anglesey's limestones are marine sedimentary rocks which were formed in relatively warm and shallow seas some 350 million years ago. Their most important chemical constituent is calcium carbonate, or calcite. Many marine plants and animals extract calcite from the sea water. They also secrete it and, when they die, their skeletons accumulate on the sea floor where, over millions of years, the skeletal material petrifies while calcite cements the whole mass together into solid rock.

The tenth stage of the walk is conducted almost entirely through limestone country. Of all the different rocks in Anglesey, Carboniferous Limestone, with its distinctive array of fossils, is probably the easiest to identify. Seaward outcrops tend to be dramatic, with sheer, jointed cliff faces that look as though they might

have been built of 'Lego', while inland outcrops can look like man-made battlements. As already seen in Lligwy Bay, where sea waves have attacked the cliffs, the limestone fractures naturally along rectangular lines, a characteristic that makes it one of man's favourite stones for building purposes.

Eastwards towards Moelfre the cliff-top path is easy going. Down below on Lligwy's sands, young families with their windbreaks, air-beds and buckets and spades add colour. Verdant farmland lies on the other side of the fence. The path then makes a dog's leg around Porth Forllwyd, an interesting little bay from which, years ago, small craft loaded limestone destined to become city architecture in Dublin and Liverpool. Vast slabs of limestone at the water's edge form near-horizontal ledges, ideal perches for a bit of fishing but, with nothing to catch hold of, absolutely deadly for anyone struggling to get ashore through heavy seas. A little way ahead, the cliffs give way briefly to a beach of limestone cobbles at Porth Helaeth, below a small caravan site. Near the beach, there is the simplest of stone monuments in a field above the path. Its equally simple inscription tells of the terrifying wreck of the *Royal Charter* on the rocks below, in a ferocious storm during the night of 25 October 1859, when 460 passengers and crew perished.

From the little cliff-top caravan site, the path leads out towards a low grassy headland and Ynys Moelfre comes into view, scene of another dramatic casualty, precisely one hundred years and one day after *Royal Charter*. Thanks to the valiant efforts of the Moelfre lifeboatmen, all eight members of the crew of the cargo ship SS *Hindlea* were miraculously saved.

Delightful little sea-front cottages provide a picturesque welcome to Moelfre, largely unspoiled by tourism, in its superbly sheltered setting. It was herring fisheries in the winter months that established and maintained the village up until the Second World War. Its seafaring tradition ran deep, with Moelfre men serving world-wide in Liverpool ships but returning home on leave to scrape, paint and launch their little clinker-built boats in readiness for the herring season and, of course, crewing the lifeboat. Moelfre's famous lifeboat station has been operational for a hundred years and is one of the first buildings to greet walkers from Lligwy Bay.

Fishermen's herring boats, drawn up on Moelfre's little shingle beach, have been replaced by dinghies and other small pleasure craft but, in reality, little has changed along the waterfront in a hundred years. The public house has been joined by cafés and an ice-cream kiosk in providing a range of refreshments for those contemplating the next short step to Traeth Bychan.

Almost from the centre of the village, the coastal path sets off in a southerly direction along low cliffs and the best views are those farewell glances back to Moelfre. The route to Traeth Bychan includes a small pebbly beach, the narrow road to Nant Bychan and neat pathways between caravan sites and fields.

Traeth Bychan is horseshoe-shaped, no more than half a mile across and completely walled in by limestone. High tide fills the bay and so coastal-path

Fossilised coral at Traeth Bychan

walkers must then follow signs from the car park, around the head of the bay, but as the tide ebbs, an enviable stretch of sand is revealed. Traeth Bychan is a safe and very popular venue for boating people, mostly small craft, sail and power. On the north side of the bay there is a small sheltered dock within old quarry workings, occupied mainly by powerboats, but it dries out at about half tide. A pleasant walk across the sands awaits and, for those interested in fossils and other aspects of the limestone environment, inspection of the rocks and the fossiliferous boulders around the bay can be very rewarding. A nicely kept path edges a development of holiday homes on the southern side of the bay and it leads out to a headland known as Penrhyn where there is a strange series of sandstone pipes penetrating the limestone. From the path, there is a good view down over the bay's pristine sands and it is difficult to relate this charming picture to the

mournful scene here in 1939 when the submarine HMS *Thetis* was beached upon these same sands, having failed to surface from her hand-over trials in the Irish Sea. All ninety-nine men on board lost their lives.

From Penrhyn the path turns south for Benllech. It climbs to the top of high limestone cliffs again and more or less remains at this level until Benllech. In contrast with the other cliff-top paths, this mile-and-a-quarter stretch closely follows the precipitous cliff edge and yet the view of the sea, and the rocks below, is restricted by vegetation. Bracken and fern soon give way to quite dense thickets of blackthorn, hawthorn and hazel, shaped by on-shore winds to give the cliff edge a rounded appearance. In several places, the route becomes a gloomy tunnel through the bushes with only hart's tongue fern and ivy able to survive in the low light. But nearing Benllech, the path opens up again to give some fine long-range views across Red Wharf Bay to Llanddona and Ynys Seiriol (Puffin Island). Toward both ends of this path, holiday homes of various types sit just beyond the inner fence, mostly arranged in neat rows, all facing south.

Many people believe that tourism created Benllech, but this is not strictly true. Quarrymen and their families founded the village while seeking high-quality building material within the Carboniferous Limestone there. It is for this reason that the village was not centred directly upon the coast. But, once the heavy blocks of limestone were hewn, they then had to be dragged or carted down to the sands as the only means of transport was by sea. Vessels would arrive on the tide, dry out on the sands as the tide ebbed, load the stone and then sail again when refloated by the next tide. But the scene was about to change, for in 1908, the village became a railhead. Now locomotives could haul the stone, and fishermen began to land their catches at Benllech for speedy delivery to market by rail. The same track brought many visitors to the village and the rest, as they say, is history. Proper roads followed the railway, English visitors came by car, liked the fabulous sands at Benllech, built their retirement and holiday homes and stayed. Caravans followed in droves and that erstwhile quarrymen's village became today's extensive resort where the railway is just a memory.

The small harbour, Traeth Bychan

Sand sculpture at Traeth Bychan

Charles Dickens and the *Royal Charter*

'The tide was on the flow, and had been for some two hours and a half; there was a slight obstruction in the sea within a few yards of my feet . . .

'O, reader, haply turning this page by the fireside at Home, and hearing the night wind rumble in the chimney, that slight obstruction was the uppermost fragment of the Wreck of the Royal Charter, Australian trader and passenger ship, Homeward bound, that struck here on the terrible morning of the twenty-sixth of this October, broke into three parts, went down with her treasure of at least five hundred human lives, and has never stirred since.'

Charles Dickens, *The Uncommercial Traveller*

CHARLES DICKENS

✠ Born in Hampshire on 7 February 1812

✠ Father imprisoned for debt in the Marshalsea Prison

✠ Worked in a blacking factory, aged twelve, to support his family

✠ Worked as a clerk in a legal practice

✠ Became court stenographer (shorthand writer)

✠ Began journalistic career in 1834 and travelled Britain by stagecoach

✠ Visited Anglesey in 1859 and reported the wreck of the 'Royal Charter'

✠ Recorded how the Rector of Llanallgo cared for those who died

✠ Died on 9 June, 1870 and is buried in Poets' Corner, Westminster Abbey, London

On the wallpath!

Red Wharf Bay

Forgotten dreams

The coastal path descends to a limestone ledge at the north end of Benllech sands, skirts a restaurant and joins a very short promenade. Ahead lies Trwyn Dwlban, a low headland that separates Benllech Bay from Red Wharf Bay and is completely occupied by a private holiday camp. At high tide, there is no safe way round it to seaward, and so, if the tide is in, there is no alternative but to follow the coastal path inland, around the back of the holiday camp, to emerge again in Red Wharf Bay. The inland route is pleasant but walking around Trwyn Dwlban along the sand is a more interesting and enjoyable way to enter the bay. Upon the dipping limestone beds at the headland, with their glacial striations (parallel scratches), there's another area of intriguing sandstone pipes – much larger than those at Traeth Bychan.

This is a good place to appreciate the great extent of Red Wharf Bay, almost two square miles of sand at low water, stretching southward towards Pentraeth and all the way across to Llanddona. The bay may have earned its Welsh name, Traeth Coch, at the time of the Vikings' plundering raids on Anglesey in the twelfth century. Their attack here led to a particularly fierce battle; casualties were high on both sides and much blood was spilled upon the sands, reportedly turning the whole bay red.

At the entrance to the bay, Castell-mawr is the first and most prominent feature to catch the eye. This very large cube of limestone rock was once the site of an early fortress, and limestone was quarried in these parts to provide stone for the Edward I castles at Beaumaris and Caernarfon. It is a surprise to learn that Red Wharf was an important centre for Anglesey trade in the eighteenth and early nineteenth centuries and that Porthllongdy was quite a busy little port. Modest levels of shipbuilding and fishing were additional activities. Shelter from the prevailing winds was the bay's main advantage and there were short-lived plans to develop the port, but it is difficult to imagine serious commercial shipping using this bay. In the past, however, high tides almost reached the village of Pentraeth, suggesting that there was a greater depth of water than there is today. Changes in sea level, uplifting, silting (or all three) could have been responsible for the reduction in depth.

A shoreline of cottages and houses, a restaurant and the Ship Inn, upturned dinghies on the spit, a few pleasure craft moored in the pool and the rest high and dry on the sands all make for a picturesque sight, an altogether pleasant place to be. South of the inn, the shore route becomes rather muddy and, in any case, is not practical at high tide; the elevated footpath to the head of the bay passes behind a few shore-side dwellings with highly-desirable views. Red Wharf Bay has a varied population of sea birds, wildfowl, waders, larks and bunting, both resident and migrant. Wind, waves and tidal currents produce many interesting sand formations and, for seashells, it is a collector's paradise. Revelling in the space and freedom are horse riders, dog walkers, cockle pickers, bikers and even the occasional sand-yachtsman! But everyone must remain alert to the speed of the incoming tide across the sands, to avoid the danger of being cut off. Out of sight from the bay, but only a mile distant, is the ancient village of Pentraeth. It is historically famous for the Battle of Pentraeth in 1170 when Hywel ap Owain Gwynedd, the Poet Prince, was slain, and again in 1859, when Charles Dickens stayed there on his way to report on the *Royal Charter* disaster. The village has always benefited from being on the old post road to Holyhead and from its proximity to Porthllongdy.

A few isolated properties mark the present line of high water at the head of Red Wharf Bay and then the route turns to the east as it crosses a small stone bridge over Afon Nodwydd which is little more than a stream. The southern side of the bay is fringed by a narrow strip of farmland and two or three farmhouses that back onto Mynydd Llwydiarth, a low range of forested hills that continues eastward to Wern farm.

Red Wharf Bay at low tide

The coastal path follows the edge of the beach but, upon reaching a marshy area, the route switches to the top of a large stone wall for at least quarter of a mile. The wall, which separates farmland from the marshy shore, has had its top levelled and concreted to provide a pathway of between two and three feet in width. In places, it must be ten feet high. At the end of the wall, the path crosses a stretch of sand, reeds and grass before joining a single-track road that leads to Pentre-llwyn, passing several interesting properties on the way, all looking onto the superb beach below this hamlet. The much larger village of Llanddona stands about 400 feet above the sea, but this was not high enough to protect inhabitants from the unwelcome attentions of a group of castaways who landed and settled on the shore below Llanddona and proved to be a thoroughly bad lot. Most feared of all were their womenfolk, whose infamy as the Witches of

Llanddona became a part of Anglesey folklore. To follow the shoreline from Trwyn Dwlban in the west around to Saint Dona's church at the eastern extremity of the bay is a walk of a good four and a half miles; Traeth Coch is Anglesey's largest bay.

From the eastern end, the coastal path threads through some boulders on the beach and then turns up into a field behind Saint Dona's church. The route is well marked and winds its way upward via several lanes, passing a number of pleasant cottages on the way. It is quite a climb but pauses for breath are rewarded with wonderful views over Red Wharf Bay and as far back as Point Lynas. On levelling out, the path runs through a large field and then joins a track that passes between farm buildings before linking into a narrow road skirting clockwise around the north side of Bwrdd Arthur (Arthur's Table), passing dwellings and a tiny church tucked under the limestone 'table'. At this point, the 'white tern' of the coastal-path sign surprisingly ignores Arthur and flies off to the east. The only way up to Bwrdd Arthur from here is to complete the circuit and find the path up through the gorse to the summit.

There is, however, an alternative. Leaving Saint Dona's church behind, in the hamlet of Pentre-llwyn, a steep and narrow road climbs north-eastwards up to a T-junction at the top of the hill, level with the tall radio and television mast that has been in view for several miles. The aerials on the mast pick up signals from transmitters elsewhere in the British Isles, then amplify and reradiate them to homes in north-west Wales. After a left turn at the T-junction onto the Penmon road, a narrow path leads up through the gorse to Bwrdd Arthur, from where there are the most glorious views in all directions. 2,000 years ago, an Iron Age fortress stood upon this site and other artefacts suggest that Romans too enjoyed the views.

Razor shell

Sunset over Red Wharf Bay

XI From Bwrdd Arthur to Beaumaris

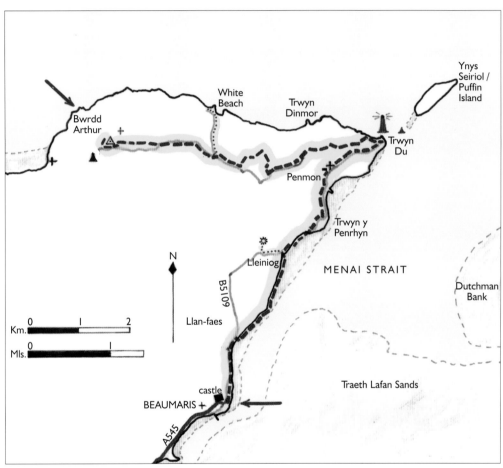

In which we walk down to Trwyn Du and the lighthouse marking the Strait's northern entrance. We learn about Saint Seiriol's Christian cell at Penmon, about raiders and devastation, and about an Augustinian Priory and its eventual dissolution. We conclude with a Strait-side walk towards Beaumaris with splendid views of the Carneddau across the water.

Deer Park wall

Modern hay-baling

Old Man's Beard

A triangulation point stands on Arthur's Table, about 540 feet above sea level, the highest point in eastern Anglesey; views include the lighthouse at Trwyn Du three and a half miles away, just south west of Ynys Seiriol (Puffin Island). This stage starts with a country walk that, for the most part, is half a mile from the severe cliffs that run from Red Wharf Bay to Trwyn Du. This is limestone country again after the brief interlude along the southern shore of Red Wharf Bay. Indeed, from Pentre-llwyn to Trwyn Du, together with off-lying Puffin Island, the rock is continuous Carboniferous Limestone. Three disused but very large coastal limestone quarries in this area bear witness to the popularity of the material for building purposes. Huge quantities of quarried stone were loaded into barges and towed to different destinations. Locally, the

two bridges spanning the Menai Strait were obvious recipients but, in terms of quantity, exports to Liverpool for the construction of city-centre buildings and harbour works were far greater.

Eastwards along the narrow Penmon road the scene is rural: homesteads, livestock and the distant mountains of Snowdonia. The elevation is between 300 and 400 feet on the road and gives an open-air, on-top-of-the-world feeling. A hundred yards beyond the turning for Glan-yr-afon and Llangoed, a lane leads north to Fedw Fawr and White Beach. It is an easy walk down the lane to a small car park and lookout, high above the shore. White Beach takes its name from the milky-coloured limestone cobbles forming the beach in this pleasant and sheltered cove. It's a favourite place with fishermen, spinning for mackerel off the headlands in July and August.

Back up the hill to rejoin the narrow Penmon road, but only for quarter of a mile before a tern-sign suggests a detour to the north and east that includes woodland, lanes with high hedges, unexpected and hidden-away cottages, fields with inquisitive ponies, and a final rendezvous with the Pentir road. The hedges around these parts, in September, are laden with rose-hips, hawthorn berries, sloes, elderberries, and blackberries, a rich harvest for the 'jam-making' pickers and an appealing sight. After half a mile the road terminates in Pentir and the route then shares some large, open fields with sheep and cattle. A magnificent limestone wall, at least eight feet high, encloses Penmon Deer Park, after which a well-made pathway leads through thorn bush and bracken, down to the cliffs, caves and cobbles that make up the most attractive and very popular Trwyn Du (Black Point) area. There is a striking view over the sound that runs between the headland and Puffin Island, with the lighthouse and red perch marking the edges of the channel from the Irish Sea into the Menai Strait. The setting is entirely limestone in character.

Though Puffin Island is not on the route, it definitely 'belongs' to this eastern extremity of Anglesey and is tantalisingly close. Famed for its association with Saint Seiriol, Vikings, semaphore signals and sea birds, Puffin Island briefly hosted a laboratory for biologists, a forerunner to today's splendid School of Ocean Sciences at Menai Bridge.

The privately-owned Trwyn Dinmor quarry is hidden from view around the promontory to the west, while the abandoned Flagstaff quarry lies concealed to the south but there is ample evidence of limestone in the topography of the headland. Precise, dipping beds of limestone run out to sea and are echoed in the rocks of Puffin Island. To the east, in front of the old coastguard houses, there are large ledges of the rock while, across the bay, there is a spectacular storm beach of limestone cobbles. Cobbles and pebbles are features of steep beaches and the different terraces are formed by the action of waves over varying tide levels. Trwyn Du lighthouse, now solar-powered and automatic, was built in 1838 following a spate of wrecks around the entrance to the Menai Strait, including the breaking up of the *Rothsay Castle* in 1831, in heavy seas with the loss of over a hundred passengers and crew.

Limestone cobbles at Penmon

Trwyn Du lighthouse flashes a white light every five seconds, visible for fifteen miles, and its fog bell is struck every thirty seconds. At high tide, the lighthouse appears to stand well out in the sound, tempting those unfamiliar with the area to take the shorter, inshore route. This could well lead to disaster on the submerged rocks and explains why the lighthouse displays the NO PASSAGE LANDWARD warning.

The lighthouse marks a change of direction for the walk to parallel the Menai Strait once again. A south-westward lane leads up and over the hill to Penmon Priory. Seiriol, one of Anglesey's better-known saints, set up a cell at Penmon (later extending his monastic settlement to Ynys Seiriol, also known as Ynys Lannog, Priestholm and Puffin Island). There is a charming legend about Saint Seiriol and his good friend Saint Cybi. Apparently, they met on a regular basis at Llannerch-y-medd, roughly midway between

Caergybi and Ynys Seiriol. Even on horseback, this was quite a journey for both of them and involved an early morning departure, and an evening return. Local people became used to this routine but questioned why Saint Cybi was always dark-tanned whereas Saint Seiriol looked pale. It was then realised that Saint Cybi faced the rising sun on his outward journey and the setting sun on his way home. Conversely, the sun warmed Saint Seiriol's back on both of his journeys and this is why they became known as 'Cybi the Tawny' and 'Seiriol the Fair'!

Saint Seiriol's sixth-century cell at Penmon was established adjacent to a well which, echoing pre-Christian Celtic religions, was believed to have special healing powers. Converts to Christianity were baptised at this well, which can be seen to this day, albeit rebuilt in the eighteenth century: just a simple rectangle of very clear water above a bed of shimmering pebbles within a tiny stone-benched shelter. The holy places at Penmon and Ynys Seiriol continued to thrive over hundreds of years until devastated during the tenth-century Viking raids. Bent upon larceny and destruction, the pagans left the monastery and its wooden church in smouldering ruins but they failed to eradicate the memory of Christianity. Recovery took a number of years, as money had to be raised, but then stone masons in the eleventh century built the cruciform church we see today in the name of 'Saint Seiriol'. Less than a hundred years later, under the direction of Llywelyn the Great, the site was transformed into a priory for Augustinian monks. Dissolution of the monasteries in 1537 finally terminated Penmon's religious associations except for the old church that has remained in use throughout. Among the contents of the church, which was last rebuilt in 1855, are two tall stone crosses that are believed to have stood at the entrance to the original monastery grounds. The prior's house is now a private residence but as for the monks' three-storeyed quarters, only the shell of the building remains. Nothing appears to have disturbed the monks' fish-pond, and lastly, a more recent yet quite sympathetic structure is the thousand-nest dovecot, built around 1600 to provide dainty morsels for the table of the local landowner who had also acquired the priory's land for his deer park. There is much to explore and ponder in this magical place but it is time to move on.

Coastguard houses in silhouette

Penmon limestone at sunrise

Strange events on Ynys Lannog

'Close to Anglesey and almost adjoining it, there is a small island inhabited by hermits, who live in the service of God by the labour of their hands. They are remarkable in that, should they have ever quarrelled with each other for reasons of human frailty, a species of small mice, which abound on the island, consume most of their food and drink, and befoul the rest. As soon as their argument is over, the plague of mice disappears immediately . . .'

Giraldus Cambrensis,
The Journey through Wales

GIRALDUS CAMBRENSIS

✠ Also known as Gerallt Gymro and Gerald of Wales

✠ Born at Manorbier castle, of mixed Norman and Welsh blood c.1146

✠ Studied at Paris after an ecclesiastical education at Gloucester

✠ Appointed chaplain to Henry II in 1184

✠ In 1188 accompanied Archbishop Baldwin on a recruitment campaign for the Third Crusade

✠ Wrote 'The Journey through Wales', an idiosyncratic account of his trip

✠ Visited Anglesey on Monday, 11 April 1188

✠ Aspired to be Bishop of St Davids but never achieved his ambition

✠ Died in Lincoln in 1223

The walk down the road from the priory toward Trwyn y Penrhyn, converging with the Menai Strait, is very pleasant. The view north-eastward, back up Penmon beach, shows a covering of limestone cobbles and pebbles. There is a substantial old jetty and, beyond that, various crumbling buildings associated with the huge, cavernous and now overgrown Flagstaff quarry. However, limestone and its influence on the beach is about to give way to mud and sand, although the characteristic high limestone walls are still in evidence on the other side of the road, dividing low-lying land into large green fields. As the road rounds Trwyn y Penrhyn and turns inland, tide permitting, walkers can leave the road and follow the sandy beach to where Afon Lleiniog, hardly more than a stream, flows down onto the beach adjacent to a small picnic car park. Less than half a mile west from the car park and close to the stream, stands another piece of history in the shape of a steep motte and bailey castle known as Castell Aberlleiniog. Now hidden by trees, the original structure was built by the Earl of Chester around 1090 as part of a Norman plan to control north Wales, but Gruffudd ap Cynan had other ideas for he captured the castle, along with its garrison, and forced the Normans to retreat. The timber fortifications were then replaced by a castle of stone but little of it remains today apart from the crumbling turrets. Early maps show Afon Lleiniog to have been a small estuary in those days, raising the probability that the castle was serviced from the sea. Today, this looks improbable but an identical situation exists at Beaumaris castle: experts suggest that, rather than a fall in sea level, sediment is the culprit, slowly silting up Anglesey's bays and estuaries and thereby reducing water depths, clogging earlier waterways and leaving the castles remote from the sea.

The walk around Anglesey's coastline reveals many different rocks exposed by the action of the sea. But in this present location, between Trwyn y Penrhyn and Beaumaris, there is little solid rock to be seen. The coastline here is of glacial origin, akin to what would be found inland where much of the solid rock is covered by deep glacial deposits and topsoil. There are some interesting geological features, however, the most obvious being the massive boulders scattered along the muddy beach below. These lumps of rock, which are a bit of a nightmare for local boat sailors, are known as 'glacial erratics' and are not native to

Blackberries

Fife sailing yachts at Beaumaris

this shore. They were carried here by an ice sheet and some have come from as far afield as Cumbria or even Scotland. Only when the ice melted did their journeys come to an end, here in the Menai Strait. More than one ice sheet passed this way, as is evident in the cliffs of glacial drift a little way south of Afon Lleiniog. The colour of the deposit depends upon its origin and careful examination of these cliffs shows that a relatively dark-coloured deposit is overlain by a lighter colour. The darker material is mainly ground-down igneous rock, deposited here by the Snowdonia ice sheet, whereas the lighter reddish-coloured deposit arrived later with the Irish Sea ice sheet.

Fryars Bay affords some grand views across the Strait to the Carneddau range of mountains, 3,000 feet high and more; quite a contrast to the rather flat Anglesey terrain. Also, if the tide is low, the huge extent of the Dutchman Bank and of the Lafan Sands becomes evident; quite a surprise. The route now joins the B5109 road to Beaumaris, and passes a wide slipway built during the Second World War to launch the Catalina flying boats that were fitted out in the Llan-faes factory across the road. The factory is no more, but the village of Llan-faes lies only a quarter-mile distant. The road walk is brief because ahead lies another glacial feature, a drumlin that looks rather like a whale's back, and the coastal path takes us to its grassy summit. Drumlins are mounds of boulder clay that were moulded into shape by advancing ice, but this one has lost its eastern half, eroded by the waters of the Menai Strait. From the top of the drumlin, there is a good view down upon the castle and town of Beaumaris, such as Edward I must have enjoyed 700 years ago.

XII From Beaumaris to Menai Bridge

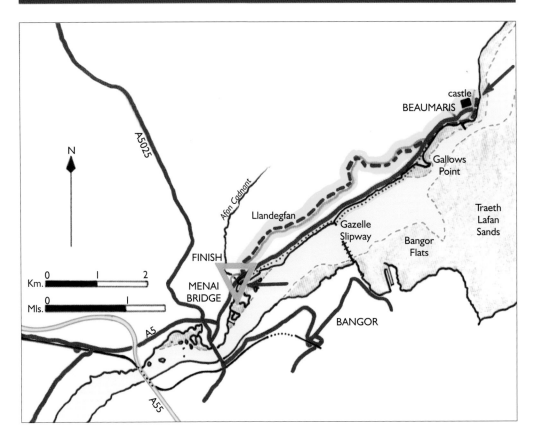

In which we focus principally on Beaumaris. We hear how Edward I evicted the citizens of Llan-faes to accommodate his planned castle and the inevitably 'English' township that followed. We learn of the town's architecture and administrative functions: its customs house, fishery office, and its role as principal port of Anglesey. Then at the end of our 125-mile walk, we return to our starting place, the bridge at Afon Cadnant.

Castle dock

Sea front at Beaumaris

Launching the lifeboat

On the way down from the top of the drumlin, there is a fine prospect, with the town sandwiched between the once-mighty castle and a spacious green that leads to a wooden pier extending into the waters of the Strait. Long ago, small communities of fishermen gave rise to most if not all of the coastal towns and villages around Anglesey, but not Beaumaris whose origin is unique and entirely the responsibility of the Norman king Edward I. As part of his ambitious plan to control the Welsh by means of a chain of coastal castles, Edward decided that his last and most powerful castle should be built upon the '*beau marais*', or beautiful marshland that fell within the boundaries of Llan-faes. His choice of a marsh for such an immense building project seems strange except that it was essential to be able to service the castle directly from the sea. The tide would have

reached the marsh and castle until more recent sediment movements silted up the approaches.

Towards the end of the thirteenth century, Llan-faes was quite an important commercial centre and port. It also catered for travellers making the difficult crossing to and from the mainland via ferry and the Lafan Sands. Additionally, a friary had been founded there in 1237 by Llywelyn Fawr. But none of this mattered to Edward I. He felt that the inhabitants of Llan-faes were too close for comfort to his intended castle and so he had them evicted in 1291 to Rhosyr in the south of Anglesey, naming the location 'Newborough'. This cleared the way for construction of the castle in 1295, an enormous symmetrical limestone and sandstone structure with fortification provided by a pair of concentric walls. The castle also had a moat and a small dock from which sea-going vessels could discharge supplies directly, through a small protected opening in the wall. Building work continued for thirty-five years but even then, the castle was not completed to its original design.

Beaumaris castle, always seen locally as a symbol of English oppression, saw some action during Owain Glyndŵr's fifteenth-century rebellion, in what proved to be the last attempt to regain Welsh independence. It also served as a prison from time to time and held some notable prisoners but, from the beginning of the sixteenth century, it ceased to have any real purpose and began to deteriorate, particularly as it was seen as a source of valuable building materials. Not until the early twentieth century did the State come to its rescue, having realised the castle's historic significance and its potential value to tourism, for it would always be a dominant feature in the town. Back in 1560, recognising that Beaumaris, with its population of 800 people, was the largest port in Anglesey, Elizabeth I issued a charter specifying the trading rights of its merchants. A custom house and fishery office were established and many vessels were registered in Beaumaris. Vessels of 12-40 tons traded to and from ports in England, Ireland and as far afield as Spain and Newfoundland. Outward cargoes consisted of agricultural produce and fish, but homeward cargoes were of a surprising variety, including wine, sugar, coal, calico, barley, prunes, figs, rice, candle-wax, salt, malt, furniture, pewter, spinning wheels, shoes and even bricks from Antwerp. Clearly the quality of life in Anglesey was improving rapidly! Beaumaris also became the centre for administration of law and order on the island. This is very interesting because certain well-known Anglesey individuals were engaged in piracy. Yet, with letters of marque from the Queen, the products of their piracy could be landed legally at Beaumaris on payment of a percentage to the crown!

Coastal-path signs point along the promenade but further exploration is needed to appreciate the castle and today's elegant seaside town. There is a pleasant mixture of every architectural era from medieval to Victorian, ranging from picturesque cottages to tall and

Christmas lights in Beaumaris

dignified houses. The town is a major attraction for visitors who naturally come to see the great castle but who will enjoy the other historic buildings, including the fourteenth-century parish church of Saint Mary and Saint Nicholas, the court-house of 1614 and the 1829 gaol. Quality shops, restaurants, public houses and hotels adequately provide for visitors' needs. Yet a great many people come simply to enjoy a happy day in pleasant surroundings, perhaps taking in a boat-trip around Puffin Island or just fishing for crabs from the pier. Local people are active in staging exhibitions, fairs, events and a festival, all contributing to the town's lively atmosphere. Row upon row of pleasure craft are moored in Beaumaris Bay during the season and members of the local yacht club engage in serious but friendly competition in their beautiful boats, staging regattas and maintaining the town's long sailing tradition.

Framing Beaumaris

Although Beaumaris castle remained under construction for thirty years, it was never actually completed. As a fortification, however, it was most efficient and could be defended by a comparatively small garrison. Surrounded moat, its two massive concentric walls linked numerous towers so that, in the unlikely event of an invader penetrat the outer wall, he would then come under devastating cross-fire from archers in at least two of the inner towers.

The employment and protection afforded by the castle soon attracted settlers, predominantly the English. Watt daub houses, with allotments, began to appear south-west of the castle, with ninety burgesses registered in 1296. T earliest of the medieval buildings surviving today are the parish church, the tiny Tudor Rose and the Bull's Head in Castle Street, originally built in the fourteenth and fifteenth centuries.

The town prospered and expanded rapidly. The sixteenth and seventeenth centuries saw construction of a tow three more inns and a court-house, while local benefactor David Hughes founded a free grammar school.

The eighteenth and nineteenth centuries found Beaumaris starting to v as an important trading centre, yet flourishing in other respects. New chu of various denominations were built or planned, the social well-being of town was invigorated through the launch of several societies, the first sai regatta was staged in 1830 and a lifeboat service was established at Penn With the population nearing 1,600 persons and the first paddle steamers arriving from Liverpool carrying visitors, elegant new buildings in the Georgian style were being constructed: Victoria Terrace, the Williams-Bu Hotel and a new gaol in Bunker Hill Lane.

Similar trends continued through the twentieth century with the found the Beaumaris Arts Festival and the town band, the building of a Catholi church and an open-air swimming pool. Today Beaumaris continues to modernise and has become an important tourist attraction, with its castl as a United Nations World Heritage Site. It has boats, beaches and beaut views but its real enchantment lies in the relics of its noble past.

The Bulkeley Hotel

1294

Any doubts that Edward I might have had about the need for a castle at Beaumaris to maintain order were quickly dispelled when the people of Anglesey rose against him in the Madog rebellion. A vibrant township subseqently developed, with marks of its long history still evident today.

1403

Owain Glyndŵr, leading the Welsh in their last war of independence, seized Beaumaris castle and held it for two years.

1642

Anglesey's Royalists garrisoned Beaumaris castle at the onset of the Civil War but they were no match for the Parliamentary forces. The last Civil War battle was fought at Red Hill, Beaumaris in 1648.

1925

The ivy-covered ruins of Beaumaris castle were placed in Government care. Today, this World Heritage Site attracts almost 100,000 visitors each year.

Castell Biwmares
Beaumaris Castle
19 87
Safle Treftadaeth y Byd
A World Heritage Site

BEAUMARIS PORT, SMUGGLERS AND PIRATES

The port of Beaumaris enjoyed a number of advantages: relatively deep water, a sheltered anchorage, proximity to major shipping routes, ferry services to mainland Wales, a local fishing industry and shipbuilding at Gallows Point. In addition, following Elizabeth I's Charter of 1562, all vessels based between Barmouth and Conwy were required to register in Beaumaris and pay their dues at the town's Custom House. At one time, there were 327 ships registered in Beaumaris compared with just eleven at Cardiff. Beaumaris-registered ships traded far and wide and the town's port activities had much to do with its growing wealth and influence, particularly as not all of these practices were legal!

The imposition of heavy duties upon tobacco, spirits and other fine goods ensured that Beaumaris would become a favoured landing place for contraband smuggled into Anglesey and north-west Wales. Smugglers' hoards were maintained in Ireland and the Isle of Man and, under cover of darkness, fishing vessels and other small sailing craft would slip into the Menai Strait carrying their illicit goods buried beneath 'innocent' cargoes of herring. Accomplices would light hilltop bonfires alerting smugglers to the location of the Revenue Cutter that patrolled Anglesey waters.

Starting in Elizabethan times, huge trading opportunities opened up across the Atlantic. Although it was Drake's activity that grabbed the headlines, piracy was not limited to French and Spanish galleons; it even spread into the Irish Sea where relatives of the Anglesey gentry joined forces with local seamen in attacking legitimate merchant vessels. Known pirates reportedly lived openly in Beaumaris and the trade in ill-gotten merchandise contributed handsomely to local prosperity.

Beaumaris Bay

Beaumaris Pier at twilight

The A545 towards Menai Bridge follows the edge of Beaumaris Bay to Gallows Point, and shares marvellous seaward views with residents of the Cae Mair estate. Gallows Point is a shingle spit protruding into the Strait and, at low water, stands at the narrowest point in the channel. Bearing in mind the history of Beaumaris, no imagination is necessary to work out how Gallows Point acquired its name. On a less macabre note, however, it was also well-known for the ships built there to help meet the demand for vessels capable of carrying cargoes of slate from Port Penrhyn and copper ore from Amlwch. No shipbuilding on the Point today but there remains a strong nautical connection with many pleasure craft stored there during the winter months, undergoing repair and maintenance in preparation for the next sailing season. And there is talk of building a marina on the south side of the Point. Until the 1950s, people could have stood on Gallows Point to watch the regular steamer from Liverpool and Llandudno heading for Menai Bridge, having already called at Beaumaris Pier. But the sight of such a passenger vessel today is rare indeed; it might just be possible to see the university's *Prince Madog* go by, with ocean-science students on a research trip, but the most likely commercial vessels are the mussel dredgers from Port Penrhyn, fishing for mussels on Bangor's mud-flats over the duration of high water.

The section of elevated road from Gallows Point to Glyn-garth is most picturesque. It twists and turns through oak and beech trees, hugging the coastline and providing lovely glimpses across the Strait. But the road carries a lot of traffic and there is no footpath. Quite rightly, therefore, the official route for the coastal footpath involves going back for a quarter mile from Gallows Point, turning up the steep hill between the church and Cae Mair and walking the roads that lead past the golf course, Pen-y-parc and through Llandegfan. This is a pleasant enough walk, with some good elevated views across the Strait, yet it seems a pity to lose the coast of Anglesey at the very end of this wonderful walk. The only alternative is to reach Gallows Point when the tide is well out, for then the beach can be walked as far as the slipway at the Gazelle Hotel. A climb back up to the road at this point ensures a safe return to Menai Bridge along the A545's footpath.

The low-water option south-westwards along the beach leads back to rocky cliffs below the road. The rock here is Gwna green-schist and it continues all the way to the suspension bridge. It has an attractive colour and there are a number of igneous dykes cutting across the host rock. There are many dykes in Anglesey, nearly all lying parallel to each other, south-east to north-west, indicating that the island was stretched at some stage, in a north-east to south-west direction. Under tension, the crustal rocks developed cracks and these were invaded by molten rock from below, which resulted in the formation of dykes. The deciduous trees above the beach put on a wonderful show of colour in autumn and, although it is not on the Anglesey shore, Bangor's long pier is a welcome and interesting addition to the view. The beach here is of stone, mud and seaweed, an ideal crustacean hideout as can be seen from the several species of crab caught in low-water traps. The Gazelle Hotel is about a mile and a quarter from Gallows Point and its adjacent slipway, until the middle of the last century, was Anglesey's landing point for the Garth ferry from Bangor. But the Gazelle remains a well-known hostelry, particularly among yachtsmen who probably find it easier to talk about their exploits than fight a losing battle against the tide!

From the road, Telford's suspension bridge is visible in the distance, a reminder that the walk has almost returned to its starting point. Indeed, once back on the A545, only a mile and a half remains. Plas Rhianfa, built originally for the Verney family in the nineteenth century, with its picturesque turrets reminiscent of Glamis castle in minature, is unmistakable among numerous elegant properties hereabout, whether viewed from the road or from the Strait. On the road itself, normal traffic seems heavy and noisy after the peace of the coastal path.

The great walk around Anglesey is complete at the Cadnant bridge. It has been a privileged and unforgettable experience – all that remains is the pleasure of revisiting some of the locations and the prospect of starting the entire walk all over again, but in the opposite direction.

Plas Rhianfa

*Jellyfish (Cyanea Lamarcki)
drifting by the Cadnant*

Acknowledgements

First of all, my thanks go to Siân Pari Huws for finding the time in her very busy life to write the foreword to *All Around Anglesey*.

My general knowledge of Anglesey has been accumulated during the last half century but it was only when I set out to write a book about the island that I realised how little I really knew. I am indebted therefore to all those who provided information and assistance in putting this book together and wish to thank: Laura Arridge, Tudor and Gwyneth Jones, Eira Pari Huws, Margaret Wood, Brian Jones, Stewart Campbell, Rosie Frankland, Terry Williams, Barbara Sadler, Gwyndaf and Elizabeth Hughes, Rodney Pace, Margaret Evans, Elfed Jones, Nick Holyfield, Eluned Stephen and Glynne Pritchard.

Anglesey is the subject of several locally written books which pre-date my own endeavours and I would like to thank the following authors whose works have enlightened me: Wendy Hughes, *Anglesey Past & Present* (Gwasg Carreg Gwalch, 1999); Margaret Wood, *Rhoscolyn Anticline* (Seabury Salmon & Associates, 2004); Bryan D Hope, *A Curious Place* (Watch House Books, 1994); Margaret Hughes, *Anglesey from the Sea* (Gwasg Carreg Gwalch, 2001) and *Anglesey Lighthouses & Lifeboats* (Gwasg Carreg Gwalch, 2004); Mike Smylie, *Anglesey & Its Coastal Tradition* (Gwasg Carreg Gwalch, 2000).

I would also like to express my gratitude to Gomer Press of Llandysul and particularly to Mairwen Prys Jones and Viv Sayer for their direction, advice and friendship.

Finally, but of the greatest importance, my thanks go to my wife Shirley and to our family for their continued belief in the project, their help at all stages and their unending support.

TRB

The author and publishers would like to thank the following for permission to reproduce pictures in this volume: the Archives Department, Bangor University (broadsheet ballad, p 105); Mike Davies, Cadoxton (photograph, p 73); Henry Jones-Davies (portrait of Owain Glyndŵr, p 139).

The poem 'A Bay in Anglesey', from *Collected Poems*, by John Betjeman © 1955, 1958, 1962, 1964, 1968, 1970, 1979, 1981, 1982, 2001 is reproduced by permission of John Murray (Publishers) Limited.